MY DAD,
THE BABE

MY DAD, THE BABE

GROWING UP WITH AN AMERICAN HERO

by
Dorothy Ruth Pirone

with
Chris Martens

QUINLAN PRESS
Boston

Published by Quinlan Press
131 Beverly Street, Boston, MA 02114

Printed in the United States of America, 1988.

Photography of the Babe Ruth Scrapbook by Art Porta Studio, Inc.

Library of Congress Cataloging-in-Publication Data

Pirone, Dorothy Ruth.
  My dad, the Babe.

  1. Ruth, Babe, 1895-1948. 2. Baseball players—United States—Biography. 3. Fathers and daughters—United States—Case studies. 4. Pirone, Dorothy Ruth. I. Martens, Chris. II. Title.
GV865.R8057 1988   796.357'092'4 [B]   87-43283
ISBN 1-55770-031-1

Dedication

To my husband, Dominick;

To my children, Genevieve, Ellen, Donna and Richard;

To all my grandchildren, so that they may know their great-grandfather;

Especially to my daughter Linda—who spent many, many hours helping me—with all my love and appreciation;

And last but not least, to my son-in-law Andrew, for his humor and patience.

Acknowledgements

Chris Martens and I would like to thank all those who gave of their time and resources. My father's teammates were extremely cooperative, especially Lefty Gomez, Ben Chapman, Joe Sewell, Jimmy Reese, Bill Dickey and Mark Koenig. Charles Owen provided valuable newspapers from Babe's 1934 barnstorming tour of Japan and background material on Moe Berg. Wilburt Christman, Jack Demarest, Teddy Greck, Jr., and Dolly Ragone were all helpful in painting a vivid portrait of Dad's reclusive years in Greenwood Lake, and Mamie Ruth contributed fresh material about his formative years in Baltimore. Others who consented to be interviewed were Johnny Vander Meer, Mel Allen, Happy Chandler, Bob Lemon, Jocko Conlin, Eliot Asinof and Pat Olsen. Not to be forgotten are the patience, perseverance and secretarial skills of my daughter, Linda Pirone Tosetti, the understanding of my husband, Dominick, or the sense of humor, editorial expertise and typing skills of Cynthia Bally Martens. Thanks also go to my friend Carolyn Bostrom, for her input into our childhood memories; to Sandy Rich, for her proofreading and questions; and to the Baseball Hall of Fame in Cooperstown, for the kind permission to reproduce some photographs of my father.

Special thanks go to Warner Fusselle, who was a constant source of inspiration and information.

Both the New York Public Library and the Boston Public Library were very competent and diligent in the retrieval of old microfilm and newspapers. And, of course, no work about the life of Babe Ruth could have been completed without the aid of the wealth of previously written material: Robert Creamer's *Babe: The Legend Comes to Life*, which provided important dates, places, events and names; Fred Lieb's *Baseball as I Have Known It*; Ford Frick's *Games, Asterisks and People*; Eliot Asinof's *Eight Men Out*; *The*

Babe Ruth Story, by Babe Ruth and Bob Considine; *The Babe and I*, Claire Ruth's autobiography with Bill Slocum; *The Real Babe Ruth*, by Dan Daniel; and *Lou Gehrig: The Iron Horse of Baseball*, by Richard G. Hubler. Also, brief excerpts were taken from the following: *The Psychology of Achievement* and *My Greatest Day in Baseball*, by John Carmichael; Don Warfield and Lee MacPhail's *The Roaring Redhead*; and *The Sporting News* and *Sport Magazine*.

Six years ago, while flipping through a copy of USA Today, *I came across the following curious item: a retired
usher at Boston's Fenway Park claimed that in the early
1930s Babe Ruth had asked that he buy him two hot dogs
and a soda. Dad had never paid him back, and now the
usher was calling him a "cheap bum."*

USA Today *found out the man's address for me, and I
sent him a check for $2.00—$.25 to cover the cost of the
hot dogs and the soda and an additional $1.75 interest.*

I never did receive that cancelled check.

Dorothy Ruth Pirone

Contents

Introduction: The Roaring Twenties   1

  1   Did the Babe Really Save Baseball? . .   9

  2   The Babe's Babe 23

  3   Breaking the Rules 29

  4   Helen Help Me 39

  5   A Rude Awakening 51

  6   Claire Declares War 63

Photographs 71

  7   The Biggest Kid of Them All 89

  8   Chief Big Bat and Chief Little Bat 97

  9   *Banzai, Babu Russu!* 113

 10   The Last Straw 121

 11   Has Anybody Seen Babe Ruth? 127

Photographs 139

 12   Making Up Ground 157

 13   Intentionally Passed 165

 14   No More Encores 175

 15   The Missing Link 189

 16   Number Three Was One of a Kind . . . 197

 17   Baseball Remembers the Babe 209

 18   The Babe Ruth Scrapbook 219

 19   Life After Babe 241

MY DAD, THE BABE

Introduction

The Roaring Twenties

The Roaring Twenties, quite possibly the craziest, most hedonistic decade of the twentieth century, were bookended by two great depressions: for Red Sox fans, the selling of Babe Ruth to the New York Yankees in the first week of 1920; and the stock market crash in October of 1929, which signaled the beginning of the Great Depression. In between, however, there was anything but depression. Society had reassessed its values by the end of World War I, decided that life was meant to be lived "one day at a time," and at last emerged from its Victorian closet. The cataclysm of changing sentiment reached every aspect of American culture so rapidly that it was nearly impossible to keep pace with its effects. As the decade began, all was not well in America.

The nation found itself faced with a serious political dilemma: Should America join the League of Nations? Democrats supported President Woodrow Wilson's League, but Republicans were in favor of returning to America's traditional policy of isolation. After its 51-41 defeat in the Republican-controlled Senate, the Treaty of Peace was shelved, and a discouraged President Wilson, unable to run for a third term because of his failing health, angrily turned the country over to Warren G. Harding in November of 1920. Wilson died four years later, his dream unfulfilled.

The end of the war precipitated a flood in the workforce, and by 1920 unemployment had become one of the country's most serious problems. Even for those who had jobs, labor disputes and a severe industrial and agricultural slump brought about by the decline of wartime production served to keep the economy depressed. Agricultural wages and prices tumbled, forcing many farmers out of business. Left with little or no alternative, many of the unemployed workers in the grain states abandoned their livelihoods, uprooted their families and relocated to bigger cities in search of jobs. Consequently American cities grew at a record rate which was seven times greater than that of rural communities.

Civil rights were also at a low ebb. Numerous lynchings, floggings, burnings and kidnappings by the Ku Klux Klan led to violent uprisings across the country in 1920. The tension continued to mount in 1921, when two hundred people were killed in Tulsa, Oklahoma, in one of the worst race riots of the decade.

And finally, a flu epidemic, one of the deadliest plagues in history, had begun to loosen its grip by 1920, but not before taking the lives of over one million people in the United States alone.

Despite the internal difficulties which unsettled the country in the aftermath of the Great War, there were many causes for optimism. Women's suffrage was gained at last in 1919-20, and along with the right to vote came a new freedom and confidence. Perhaps nowhere was this change more marked than in women's fashions; shorter skirts, slimmer silhouettes and flashier accessories all were intended to glorify femininity, not obscure it.

The decade also saw a radical change in moral values. Chaperones became obsolete. Bold actresses such as Clara Bow, Greta Garbo and Gloria Swanson championed sexuality on the silver screen. But it was Rudolph Valentino who best represented the amorous desires and fantasies of post-war America as Hollywood's first "Screen Lover."

Of course, the twenties would not have been the same without music—not the battle hymns and marches that sent "our boys" overseas, but *jazz*. With the new emphasis on this lively, loose and rhythmic sound, dancing was bound to follow suit. The Charleston and the tango were not just dances, they became obsessions, and ballroom waltzes and dancing in the home were now passé.

On January 16, 1920, Prohibition went into effect, yet even this potentially crushing blow could not dampen the party atmosphere. Society had no intention of doing without alcohol, and bootleggers and speakeasies thrived.

Prohibition was by no means the only law being broken. Tales of crime and corruption were omnipresent in the headlines, and authorities seemed powerless to keep control. Gangsters such as Al Capone and Legs Diamond wreaked havoc on a vulnerable yet dissipated society. And when it was discovered in September of 1920 that the World Series of 1919 between the Chicago White Sox and the Cincinnati Reds had also been infiltrated by gamblers and hoodlums—that was the ultimate slap in the face of the nation's innocence. This revelation unceremoniously toppled baseball from its national pedestal and left in its place an image of greed and corruption. The slogan of the entire country, which had been "Play ball," was replaced with taunts of "Play bail."

With the help of two heavyweights, George Herman "Babe" Ruth, the game's first bona-fide home run hitter and gate attraction, and Judge Kenesaw Mountain Landis, its first commissioner, baseball was able to pick itself up off the canvas and come out swinging. Babe Ruth swung first, swatting fifty-four home runs in his first season for New York and adding a new dimension to the game. Landis counterpunched by banning from baseball for life the eight Chicago White Sox players who had intentionally lost the World Series.

Radio was in its fledgling stage in 1921, when Judge Landis gave permission for the first broadcast of a World Series to take place. Landis was pleased with the results and continued the experiment the following year, when the Giants and Yankees met in a rematch. Veteran sportswriter Ring Lardner, known for his sarcastic sense of humor, called Series' broadcaster Graham McNamee to task for his lack of baseball knowledge: "They played two World Series games at the Polo Grounds this afternoon—the one I watched and the one broadcast by Graham McNamee."

Radio was an instant hit with the fans but not with the owners, who felt that it posed a threat to the economics of the game; they argued that attendance would drop if fans were able to stay home and listen to games on the radio. However, it did not take long for the moguls to change their tune when they realized that sponsors were willing to spend top dollar to be part of their broadcasts. Soon Babe Ruth became the voice of the Roaring Twenties. But it was not simply his booming voice and hearty laugh coming over the airwaves; Babe's inimitable style, boundless energy, colorful personality and insatiable appetite for the carnal pleasures in life epitomized the decade. By the early 1930s every major league team had jumped on the bandwagon and was broadcasting its own games, hoping to cash in on this new form of entertainment.

In an era that demanded vibrant personalities, almost every sport responded. Boxing had Jack Dempsey, one of the most charismatic stars of the day and Babe's number-one competition for headlines. In golf it was the irascible Walter Hagen and the tempestuous Bobby Jones. The brains of Knute Rockne, the brawn of Red Grange and the versatility of the Four Horsemen of Notre Dame kept football's head above water. Bill Tilden's finesse and Suzanne Lenglen's provocative short skirts turned heads on the tennis courts. Even horseracing had an entrant into the publicity sweepstakes: Man O' War, touted as "the Racehorse of Centuries."

Baseball, of course, had its fair share of characters: Rabbit Maranville, the aging star of the Pittsburgh Pirates, was known for clowning around on hotel window ledges in the rain. And there was the effervescent and always unpredictable outfielder for the New York Giants, Casey Stengel. According to eyewitnesses, Casey one time stunned a crowd in Pittsburgh when he tipped his cap, acknowledging the cheers, and a sparrow flew out.

The larger-than-life stars gave sports fans a rare mixture of entertainment and competition. Hordes of spectators filled racetracks, golf courses, tennis courts, boxing rings, football fields and baseball stadiums. With attendance records being set in almost every sport, demands for bigger stadiums began to be heard. In some instances the shortage of seats did not deter the die-hard fans. In 1924 at Ebbets Field in Brooklyn, an estimated 100,000 fans stormed the gates with bats and tire-irons to see the first-place showdown between the New York Giants and the Brooklyn Dodgers. Since Ebbets Field only seated around 40,000, countless fans not only missed the game but also spent the next few days in the hospital, recovering from injuries suffered in the melée.

If the twenties saw the golden age of sports in America, then they also saw the golden age of sportswriters: former poets, novelists, cartoonists, humorists and war correspondents. Baseball was the sport that attracted the most gifted of the lot; and New York, home of Babe Ruth and three professional baseball teams—the Yankees, the Giants and the Dodgers—was the city that demanded their immediate attention.

There were twelve daily newspapers in New York in 1920, and competition for jobs and readers was fierce. Freddy Lieb, the dean of baseball writers, covered the game for no less than seven decades, beginning in 1911. Grantland "Granny" Rice, quite possibly the most descriptive and popular sportswriter of all-time, covered other sports besides baseball but never missed the World Series. Add to the list Shakespearean scholar John Kiernan, hard-nosed Sid Mercer, famed interviewer Frank Graham and erudite Heywood Broun, a Harvard University graduate who always looked like he had slept in his clothes. And of course there was the colorful Damon Runyon, one of the true giants of journalism. Runyon followed baseball for many years but later traded in his scorecard to concentrate on boxing, short fiction, screenplays and social commentary. Rounding out the impressive cast were Ford Frick, Bill Slocum, Rud Rennie, Dan Daniel, Joe Williams and Marshall Hunt, who was said to be at his best when he wrote about my father. Four of these men have been inducted into the Baseball Hall of Fame in Cooperstown, New York: Rice, Lieb, Runyon and Broun. With so many distinguished writers assembled in one place, the most difficult decision of the day may have been what paper to read first.

What was it about baseball that attracted so many of the country's finest writers? There was plenty of column space, ample time to meet deadlines, cooperation from the players and owners, and a demand from the American public for vivid, creative reporting, not technical accounts of the game. And there was my dad, the Babe, arguably the most quotable athlete of the century. Babe always had time for the writers. After they had exhausted every question about baseball, they would launch into other subjects: politics, women's rights, gambling, money, golf, traveling, cars, religion—you name it, they asked it. Dad was never at a loss for words, whether he understood the question or not.

Lieb wrote about Babe in 1977, "With the exception of King David of Israel, whose slingshot knockout of Goliath is recorded in millions of Bibles printed in hundreds of languages, George Herman "Babe" Ruth was the most publicized athlete who ever lived." Everything my father said or did was news; whether he blew his nose or stubbed his toe, the fans wanted to read about it. And he was always getting hurt. Dozens of writers collectively held their breath every time he was carried off the field—I believe Dad led the league in that category most seasons. He probably could have won a few awards for acting; still, the writers never grew tired of his performances. As Heywood Broun later wrote, "We gazed upon Ruth with a wonder that never grew stale."

The twenties was a time of radical change and even more radical behavior. To the best of my knowledge, Dad never swallowed goldfish, hung from flagpoles or entered any dance marathons, all ingenious ways of having a "good" time, but he probably did not miss out on much else. He always lived life at breakneck speed, with no time to waste for red lights or slaps on the wrist. Sleep was no more than a rude interruption of his busy schedule, something he did to pacify weary wives and irate managers. He never stayed in the same place or hung around with the same people for very long; he was constantly experimenting with new places, people and activities. I have often felt that if someone was able to follow my father around for one complete day, they would probably have enough material for *two* books, at least. I think the only time he took it easy was when he trotted around the bases.

When he swung, he did so with all his might, knowing that when he made contact, the results were more often than not spectacular. Fans marveled at the skilled batsmanship of Ty Cobb, Honus Wagner, George Sisler and Rogers Hornsby, as well as at their uncanny ability to elude defenders with their carefully placed hits, but never before had the fans witnessed the controlled aggression and perfectly timed swing of Babe Ruth. He was right at home on the ballfield and right at home in the Roaring Twenties. Ford Frick, one of Babe's ghostwriters, said it best: "He was the right man, in the right place, at the right time."

1

Did the Babe Really Save Baseball?

It all began on January 5, 1920, with the official announcement that the New York Yankees had purchased Babe Ruth from the Boston Red Sox. In a complicated financial deal estimated at more than $400,000, Colonel Jacob Ruppert and his partner, Colonel Tillinghast Huston, agreed to pay Harry Frazee, owner of the Red Sox, the astounding sum of $125,000. Of even greater significance was their willingness to lend Frazee $300,000, and to hold the mortgage on Fenway Park, Boston's home field. It was one of the most sensational deals in baseball history, and one that engendered a great deal of disappointment and bitterness on the part of Boston fans. The Yankees' regular appearances in the World Series throughout the 1920s would only add salt to their wounds; the Red Sox, meanwhile, would have to wait until 1946 for their next pennant.

The question on everyone's mind was, What could possibly have motivated Frazee to do such a crazy thing? After Dad's phenomenal success in 1919, the year he set a new home run record with twenty-nine in his first year in the outfield as a full-time player, he threatened to sit out the entire 1920 season if Frazee did not double his salary. Frazee was already experiencing financial difficulties, as he invested in theatrical ventures, his first love, and tried to stay one step ahead of his creditors, to whom he still owed substantial sums of money from his purchase of the team in 1916. The last thing he needed was to hear Babe's contract demands.

Frazee decided he could kill three birds with one stone by selling Babe to the Yankees. W. O. McGeehan, known for his wry wit and catchy phrases, summed it up rather neatly when he wrote, "It's the only case in all of baseball history in which a new stadium was traded for a Broadway musical production." Essentially, McGeehan was right. Frazee used part of the money to finance the production of *No, No, Nanette*, which became one of the biggest box-office smashes of the twenties. Ruppert, on the other hand, used the record gate receipts generated by Dad's home runs to construct Yankee Stadium, which appropriately was nicknamed "The House That Ruth Built" when it opened in 1923.

Shortly after the deal was completed, the Yankees signed Babe to a two-year contract which guaranteed him $41,000 for the 1920 and 1921 seasons combined. Dad was the highest paid player on the team, and he had yet to put on its uniform.

It was easy to forget, as the years passed and his home-run totals mounted, that Babe ever wore anything but a Yankee uniform; even today I meet people who think he began his career in Yankee pinstripes. Hitting has always overshadowed pitching, most fans preferring 10-9 slugfests to 1-0 pitching duels, and in Dad's case that certainly holds true.

By the time Babe died in 1948, he had established or equaled fifty-five major league records, fifty-four of which were for slugging. The fifty-fifth was for pitching, and it happened to be the record of which he was most proud: 29 2/3 consecutive scoreless innings in World Series play.

From 1915 to 1918 many experts considered Babe to be the second-best pitcher in the American League, and the "Big Train," Walter Johnson, was in a class by himself. But Dad rose to the occasion every time he faced Johnson, and at one point he beat the hard-throwing right-hander five times in a row. At the end of Dad's pitching career he held a commanding 8-2 edge in lifetime head-to-head competition against the best pitcher in American League history.

Babe was the win/loss leader in the American League in his first season as a regular in Boston's starting rotation, with an 18-8 record and a .697 winning percentage. For the following two seasons, 1916 and 1917, Dad was 23-12 (.657) and 24-13 (.649). In 1916 he had a 1.75 earned run average, the only time he led the league in that department.

He was even more impressive in World Series action. In the second game of the 1916 Series, Babe pitched fourteen innings and beat the Brooklyn Dodgers, 2-1, for what remains the longest stint by a pitcher in World Series history. The Dodgers scored their only run in the first inning on an inside-the-park home run; Dad was perfect the rest of the way. In the 1918 World Series against the Chicago Cubs, Dad pitched 16 2/3 more consecutive scoreless innings, which broke Christy Mathewson's record by 1 2/3 innings.

But by 1918 it was obvious that Babe's bat was more valuable than his arm. He still won thirteen games that year, but he also hit eleven home runs, tying Tilly Walker, an outfielder for the Philadelphia Athletics, for the league lead. It was an amazing record at the time because Dad only batted 317 times, a little over half the amount of at-bats he would have gotten in a full season. Babe only played in 97 games, mostly at first base and in the outfield when he wasn't pitching, and failed to bat in about 40 percent of his team's games.

Red Sox manager Edward Barrow recognized my father's potential as an everyday player and converted him to the outfield in 1919. At first, Babe tried to take his turn in the rotation every fourth day and play the outfield in his spare time, but it proved to be too much of a strain on his body.

The choice was simple: Babe would play the outfield full-time. It was a decision that neither of them would ever regret.

Grantland Rice remembered meeting Dad for the first time in Tampa, Florida, at the Red Sox' spring training complex. Rice watched as Babe took his first swings in the batting cage as an outfielder, not a pitcher. "After bombing about ten shots," said Rice, "Ruth circled the bases with short, pigeon-toed steps, a base-circling trot destined to become as celebrated as Man O' War's gallop." The columnist approached him as he sat in the dugout toweling off and said, "Babe, I was watching you swing. You swing like no pitcher I ever saw."

"I may be a pitcher, but first off I'm a hitter," Babe answered him. "I copied my swing after Joe Jackson's. His swing is perfect. Joe aims his right shoulder square at the pitcher, with his feet about twenty inches apart. But I closed my stance to about 8 1/2 inches, or less. I find I can pivot better with it closed. Once my swing starts, I can't change it or pull up on it. It's all or nothing at all."

This was to become one of the major turning points in Dad's career. Without having to worry about his regular turn in the rotation, Babe proceeded to pound the ball on a daily basis. And each time he approached what was *believed* to be the major league record, historians would dig up the *authentic* record. They even went back to 1884 to find that Ed Williamson had hit 27 for the Chicago Colts. But no matter how far back they combed the record books, by the middle of June it was clear that Dad had no intention of being denied. After a flurry of home runs in August, he tapered off in September but still had enough left to break Williamson's major-league record. It was appropriate that Babe's record-setting blast was hit at the Polo Grounds in New York, his future home. He ended the season with 29 home runs, 112 RBIs and a .322 batting average.

With credentials like that, Dad's stock soared around the league. Many owners were willing to open their checkbooks, but none of them could even dream of matching the

Yankees offer. Frazee was in the process of cleaning house anyway, and since Ruppert had been so cooperative, why not send the rest of his good players to him? Within two years the Yankees acquired an excellent pitching staff from Frazee: Waite Hoyt, Herb Pennock, Carl Mays, Joe Bush and Sam Jones. And as if that was not gracious enough, Frazee also parted with his manager, Edward Barrow, at the end of the 1920 season. Barrow had one of the sharpest minds for baseball and business in the history of the game. He became general manager in 1921, and chief architect of the great Yankee teams of the twenties, thirties and forties. From 1921 until 1943 the Yankees won the American League pennant fourteen times with Barrow at the helm.

Barrow and Babe would team up to win seven pennants with the Yankees, developing one of baseball's classic love/hate relationships in the process. But before their reunion in 1921, the Yankees were still hoping that George Herman "Babe" Ruth would lead the team to its *first* pennant in 1920.

Babe was off to a slow start in his first season in New York, missing five games in April with assorted injuries and failing to hit a home run. His frustrations were magnified by the impatient fans and Ruppert's critics. They wanted an instant return on New York's $400,000 investment, and it was hard to blame them. After all, Dad's price tag was more than the cost of most franchises.

Capacity crowds filled New York's Polo Grounds, anxiously awaiting the moment when my father would snap out of his doldrums and live up to his billing. Finally, on May 1, Babe hit his first home run as a Yankee, a tremendous clout that cleared the grandstand roof at the Polo Grounds and landed in the street. The following day he smashed another; this one stayed just inside the park, landing in the upper deck. This second home run in as many days sent the crowd into a frenzied celebration. Confetti rained down from the upper deck, fans climbed on the dugout, and hats flooded the field.

One hat in particular, a well-polished black derby, landed

near his feet as he crossed the plate. Babe, never one to miss an opportunity to be the consummate crowd-pleaser, replaced his Yankee hat with his newest souvenir, the home-run derby. My father's "hat trick" delighted his legion of loyal followers, and, yes, the home-run derby had truly begun.

By the middle of May Dad had five home runs and was ahead of his own record-setting pace of twenty-nine the previous year. After he hit his eighth home run on May 25, a *New York Times* headline exclaimed, "Ruthville is Babe's own kingdom, and its population is growing everyday." His home runs brought fans to the ballpark in record numbers. On May 16 the Yankees set a new attendance mark of 37,600, and the Polo Grounds had to turn away more than ten thousand fans. Those who were not fortunate enough to get tickets stood across the street from the stadium and got the details of the game by watching the scoreboard and listening to the crowd reactions. By the end of the season the Yankees had drawn 1,289,422 fans, setting a major-league attendance record.

By the beginning of June Dad was hitting home runs on an almost daily basis, exceeding even his staunchest supporters' expectations. On June 2 he swatted three in one game, a feat never before accomplished. Sportswriters were scrambling for new nicknames to best describe Babe's extraordinary hitting prowess. My two favorites were the "Caliph of Clout" and the "Mastodonic Mauler."

F. C. Lane, one of the premier baseball writers of the day, wrote in *Baseball Magazine*, "Babe Ruth is a mountain peak which towers at present above the baseball horizon." The king's ransom that Ruppert had surrendered for my father now seemed like a bargain, and the deal was being hailed as "The Steal of the Century."

Babe was not only hitting home runs more frequently than anyone in history, he was also hitting them farther and harder than anyone had ever thought possible. One writer remarked, "None of Babe's home runs have gone into the lower grandstand. He can't hit them that easy. They could use Ruth on a battleship if the ammunition runs out." The home runs were hit so far and so high that some of them were literally hit clean out of sight. Because of Dad's awesome power, it became necessary to extend the foul lines, which normally ended at field level, all the way to the roof!

Besides redefining certain physical dimensions of the game, Dad's home runs added a new dimension to the strategy of the game. More simply stated: Babe revolutionized baseball. From 1900 to 1918 scientific hitting had dominated baseball, and Wee Willie Keeler's famous saying, "Hit 'em where they ain't" was accepted by most players as the most successful approach to hitting. Scoring runs depended heavily on placement hits, bunting, stolen bases and squeeze plays. Babe changed this methodical hit-and-run approach to the more exciting game of hit . . . and trot. The birth of the big inning had arrived, and major league baseball gladly embraced it.

Dad gave the players added confidence in their abilities, and as the season progressed, everyone started swinging for the fences. Some asserted that the dramatic increase in home runs was mainly due to a "lively," or "rabbit," ball; in fact, it was widely rumored that the American League had deliberately "juiced up" the ball to showcase Babe's considerable talents and add more excitement to the game. But no concrete evidence was ever produced to substantiate these claims. The manufacturers of the two major league balls used claimed that the 1920 baseball was the same as in previous seasons. National League President John Heydler even went to the factory where the Spalding National League ball was manufactured to ensure that methods in use were the same as before. "During the war, the government commandeered the high grade of wool in the country, and private manufacturers were obliged to get along as best they could," reported Heydler. "Naturally, the quality of the ball probably declined somewhat during this period. Now that it's possible to secure the best workmanship and materials, the ball has somewhat improved." Although Heydler determined that the ball was being slightly better made, he felt that the difference was not significant enough to warrant any change in manufacturing the ball or any further investigation.

In the summer of 1919 major league baseball suffered a terrible loss when pitcher Carl Mays of the Yankees beaned Ray Chapman of the Cleveland Indians, killing him. Mays was suspended and almost forced to retire because of the tragedy. Some accused him of throwing a "trick" pitch, although he adamantly denied all such allegations. Baseball was not taking any chances and placed new restrictions on pitchers in order to avoid a repeat incident. They outlawed the "spit" ball, the "emory" ball and the "shine" ball, all common methods of "defacing a ball in order to gain more movement on it," as described by a league official. Both leagues had ignored these potentially dangerous pitches for years but now were forced to revaluate their stance for the good of the game.

Pitchers were incensed at the elimination of their trick pitches; they argued that the hitters would now have an unfair advantage over them. To make matters worse, they were handicapped by another new rule. In the past, foul balls that were hit into the stands were required to be thrown back on the field by the fans and used over again. With the new rule the crowd was allowed to keep foul balls, and if a ball was scuffed or smudged in any way, an umpire was forced to throw it out of play. Most hitters favored the new balls over the beat-up ones for the obvious reason that the new balls would travel greater distances. The pitchers felt that they were being punished as a group for the unfortunate death of Ray Chapman and loudly protested these changes; they felt that their livelihoods were being threatened, and they may have been right. Batters became less fearful of a pitch "getting away" and confidently crowded the plate, eager to challenge the "defenseless" pitcher, who had little if any recourse.

The owners pretty much ignored the feelings of the pitchers and next focused their attention on the game's most serious problem to date: gambling. It was rumored throughout 1920 that the World Series of 1919 between the Chicago White Sox and the Cincinnati Reds was fixed, but owners like Charles Comiskey of the White Sox and the governing bodies of both leagues dismissed such talk as pure folly. Nonetheless, Hugh Fullerton of the *New York Evening Record* and *Chicago Herald and Examiner* and James Isaminger of the *Philadelphia North American* conducted ongoing investigations into the matter.

As September approached, nothing substantial had been made public, and all rumors were neatly squelched. Many in baseball refused to accept the obvious for fear of the devastating effect such knowledge might have on the game. Eliot Asinof, author of *Eight Men Out*, told me, "Some of the reporters knew about the scandal, but they were hesitant to take up the controversy, because the politics in baseball didn't allow it to be published." Without the help of the writers, the owners would never have been able to suppress the story for as long as they did. And since word traveled almost solely by newspaper in 1920, a cooperative writer was a very valuable ace to have up one's sleeve.

During a normal season such glaring omissions on the part of the writers would have been conspicuous, but 1920 was the year that Dad kept the sporting world preoccupied with his record home run barrage. Also, one of the closest pennant races in American League history thankfully gave the writers something else with which to fill the headlines. By the middle of September the Yankees, White Sox and Indians were in a virtual tie for first place, and the unthinkable total of fifty home runs was well within reach of Dad's mighty 54-ounce bat.

Meanwhile, major league baseball spent most of the summer cracking down on gambling. The owners were unanimous in their belief that serious measures should be taken to rid baseball of "this terrible cancer," as one owner put it. To this end, they orchestrated numerous arrests by plainclothes detectives in almost every ballpark; the owners wanted to prove to the fans and the media that their game was clean.

However, by the beginning of September 1920, these careful efforts were proving of no avail. The grand jury of Cook County, Illinois, was prepared to open proceedings on September 7, with accusations that the Cubs-Phillies game of August 31 had been fixed by gamblers. The grand jury also announced plans to launch a full-scale investigation into the events of the 1919 World Series. And as if that was not enough, it was also rumored that the White Sox, who were in first place at the time, "were forbidden to win the pennant." The White Sox had lost six games in a row, and, as one writer put it, "They're playing an awful lot like they did when they lost the World Series."

Then, on September 24, with the grand jury ready to hand down indictments of the eight suspected White Sox players, Dad blasted his fiftieth and fifty-first home runs of the season in the first game of a double-header in New York. Unfortunately, his heroics would no longer dominate the headlines. Four days later, on September 28, baseball was dealt a dramatic knockdown blow when it was revealed on the front page of almost every newspaper in America that eight members of the Chicago White Sox had conspired with gamblers to deliberately lose the World Series for an estimated total of $100,000.

The indictments sent shock waves through the baseball community. Charles A. Comiskey suspended the eight players and conceded the pennant to the Indians. Eliot Asinof poignantly summed up the devastating effect of "the Black Sox scandal," as it had come to be known, on the psyche of the American people:

> As the impact of the confessions sank in, the American people were at first shocked, then sickened . . . . But the scandal was a betrayal of more than a set of ballgames, even more than of the sport itself. It was a crushing blow at American pride . . . . Baseball was a manifestation of the greatest of America at play. It was our national game; its stars were national heroes, revered by kids and adults alike, in all classes of society. In the public mind, the image was pure and patriotic.

The effects of the scandal promised to have long-range repercussions. Years later many players were still so ashamed that they refused to talk about it. *Baseball Magazine*, the highly acclaimed national monthly known for its in-depth stories and timely interviews, pretended the incident was nothing more than a bad dream and failed to write about it for the next two years.

The owners, on the other hand, could ill afford to ignore the problem. They desperately needed new leadership. Baseball had been governed unsuccessfully for quite some time by the National Commission, which was comprised of three men: John Heydler, president of the National League, Ban Johnson, president of the American League, and Gary Herrmann, owner of the Cincinnati Reds. In November of 1920, after much bickering amongst themselves, the owners made Judge Kenesaw Mountain Landis the game's first commissioner.

The reorganization of baseball did not come without a price. The owners practically crawled into Landis's court-room in Chicago and begged him to accept the $50,000-per-year position. By comparison, my father's brow-raising salary in 1920 was a mere $20,500.

But money was not the only sacrifice the owners had to make: Landis accepted the job only after the owners agreed to his terms. Primarily, this meant giving him absolute power to do whatever he felt was necessary to restore credibility and integrity to a decaying game. Landis was given the authority to fine clubs, expel players from games, and suspend league presidents or owners. In essence, the owners placed themselves at Landis's mercy. His stoic looks, unyielding stance and relentless pursuit of justice earned him the nickname "The Czar of Baseball."

In August of the following year, after a jury had acquitted the eight Chicago White Sox players of all charges, Landis intervened and banned the eight players from organized baseball for life, despite efforts to clear their names. One of the guilty players, "Shoeless" Joe Jackson, had been for the past ten years baseball's third leading hitter, with a lifetime batting average, including 1920, of .356. My father was so impressed with his hitting style and mechanics that he modeled his own swing after Jackson's. Ironically, at this particular time both men and their teams were headed in opposite directions. Jackson never played another game, and the White Sox, who some experts felt had had the potential of becoming a dynasty, fell flat on their faces. Conversely, Babe had just begun to flex his muscles, and the Yankees were on the verge of becoming one of the finest teams in baseball history.

The owners met Landis's landmark decision with unanimous approval. After hearing the news, one owner boasted to a group of fans that "baseball will once again be clean, now that we've gotten rid of the dirty players." Others triumphantly rejoiced, proclaiming Landis "the man who saved baseball." But some felt the credit belonged elsewhere. "All Landis did was chop off a few heads," Asinof told me. "It was Babe Ruth who saved baseball. If it hadn't been for Ruth, no one would have gone to another game. It would have taken years to heal the fans' wounds, and, quite possibly, [baseball] may never have been the same. At the time, there was a feeling that everything from a boxing match to a presidential election might be fixed. Then along comes Ruth and knocks the whole mentality out of the box. Even though everything may have been fixed, you couldn't 'fix' Babe Ruth."

Babe, like most players, was ashamed of the scandal and reluctant to talk about it at the time, yet he wrote about it in his 1948 autobiography, *The Babe Ruth Story*: "If my homerun hitting in 1920 established a new era in baseball, helped the fans of the nation, young and old, forget the past and the terrible fact that they had been 'sold out,' that's all the epitaph I want."

A quick check of the statistics from 1920 and 1921 shows that Babe had the greatest back-to-back seasons in the history of baseball. He had 54 home runs, a .376 batting average, nine triples, 137 RBIs, 158 runs scored, and a slugging percentage of .847, still the major league record. After making a mockery of the record books in his first season as a Yankee, fans were eager to see what Babe could do for an encore. He turned quite a few heads when he vowed to have an even better year in 1921. "I only played in 142 games," he said half-seriously. "Next year I'll play every game."

Babe fell short of playing in every game, but he did live up to his promise by improving in every offensive category except slugging percentage, which was a not-too-shabby .846, only one point lower than the previous year. He had 59 home runs and batted .378. He added seven triples, eight doubles, 19 runs and almost 30 hits—all while he was walked 144 times! Those two seasons are still considered the statistical finest in the history of baseball.

After two years of following Dad's daily progress for *Baseball Magazine*, F. C. Lane, one of the most insightful and respected sportswriters, frustrated at having exhausted what had seemed to be a bottomless pit of hyperbole, simply concluded: "He is Babe Ruth, the incomparable, the irresistible, the nonpareil, the only player who ever dominated baseball as though he held the vast and fascinating sport in the palm of his brawny hand."

BABE RUTH AND MRS. BABE ALL MIXED UP ON BABY'S BIRTHDAY

Dorothy Arrived June 7, 1921, Says Wife; Snookyukums Two Years Old Feb. 2, Beams Proud Father

The unique distinction of possessing two reputed birthdays is held by Baby Dorothy Ruth, curly-haired little daughter of Mr. and Mrs. Babe Ruth, whose existence was discovered for the first time on Friday, more than a year after its debut on this earth.

This curious anomaly was brought out yesterday in two varying statements by Baby Dorothy's parents.

While she was cooing with ecstasy over the baby's tiny, saucy, upturned nose, tilted in a manner similar to that of its famous home run swatting parent, Mrs. Babe, in her apartment at the Hotel Ansonia, proudly announced that the latest Ruthian edition first saw the light on June 7, 1921, in St. Vincent's Hospital.

Proud Father

"Gee, but she's a great kid!" exclaimed the great Babe as he stepped up to the plate, sighing with paternal pride. "She'll be just two years old come next February 2, and boy! make believe she won't be some baby."

Maybe the Babe had forgotten the date after all. Maybe, in the mad race for the pennant, in which his team is leading the league by only a few games, the time when home runs are most needed to cinch the flag, the Babe's thoughts wandered from that eventful day in February or June.

Then, too, parents have a way of boasting about their infants. It seems to give such a glow of satisfaction to announce to a gallery of enthusiastic admirers that one's child is twenty months old instead of sixteen. Perhaps that's how the Babe felt about it.

A Big Girl Now

Babe was unlimited in his boasting yesterday, but it was excusable, for a father who doesn't boast about his offspring is not human, that's all there is to it.

"Yep," exploded the Babe, "Dorothy's getting to be a big girl now. She weighed only three pounds when she came into this world and for a while we weren't sure the little rascal would live."

"But when we put her in an incubator she began to pick up right away and now she's just as healthy as any other kid. How is it the newspapers never heard about Baby Dorothy's birth? Well, it happened that the newspapers didn't get wind of it then and neither Mrs. Ruth nor I made any effort to make it generally known."

Tooth a Month

But despite the discrepancy in the dates given by Baby Ruth's parents as to her birthday, it seems an incontrovertible and uncontradicted fact that little bit of joy and sweetness weighs just eighteen pounds!

And she has sixteen teeth!

One little teeny-weeny tooth for each month, if we accept Mrs. Ruth's statement that her daughter is sixteen months old.

Up in the Hotel Ansonia, surrounded by all manner of delightful toys and games, was little Baby Dorothy yesterday, giving her first interview to a SUNDAY NEWS reporter, emphasizing her boos and gurgles in such manner as to do credit to a veteran.

"Nothing to Say."

Questioned repeatedly on the date of her natal day, the little darling persistently gave the same answer:

"I have nothing to say!"

She looked adorable as she lay there in her doting mama's lap, gazing with unknowing eyes on the wonderful trophies scattered about the room, telling mute tales of the prowess of her slugging father.

A mass of curls she was, curls

Babe, the proud father.

silken in texture, almost a pure white, crowning a beautifully shaped little head. And her eyes! Brown they are—big, wondrous, prettily brown, like those of her mother.

But wait! See that smile! A smile as warm as a sun's ray, suffusing everything and every one about it with unmitigated happiness.

It begins slowly, the corners of the mouth just twitching, and then, like the ripple started when a stone is thrown in the pond, expands wider and wider and then breaks out into a most delicious little coo!

Picture of Papa?

"Don't you think she is the exact image of her father?" Mrs. Ruth exclaimed. Her nose is a duplicate of my husband's. Just see how it turns up.

"She has sixteen teeth now. Aren't they just two cute for words?"

"But she can't walk," continued the adoring mother. "And all she can say is 'Mamma' and 'Da-da'." Mr. Ruth thinks the world of her. He calls her up every night on the phone, no matter where he's playing. He adores her.

"We're going to see him next week when he plays in Boston, little Dorothy and I. He told me not to dare leave her behind. She's his mascot, you know."

Three Have Died

On the mantelpiece w re photographs of three other little children. Mrs. Ruth's eye dimmed as she spoke of them.

"The first one is Helen. She died when only a few days old. That fat baby was George Jr. He was taken away when he was only four months old. Margaret left us

when she was only a year and a half.

No Record of Birth

Employes of the Ansonia say it is only recently that Dorothy has been seen at the hotel. At the Department of Health there is no record in the bureau of vital statistics of the birth of a child to Ruth and his wife in 1920, 1921 or 1922. Physicians are required to record births in New York with the Health Department.

At St. Vincent's Hospital the sister in charge of the hospital records refused to state whether Mrs. Ruth had been a maternity case at that institution on June 7, 1921.

(C) 1922: The SUNDAY NEWS: N.Y.)
(Other picture on page 1)

Increased Service on B. R. T. Subway Lines Underway Tomorrow

Increased service on B. R. T. subway lines becomes effective tomorrow, as ordered by the Transit Commission.

Under the new schedules a train will be operated every minute and a half, which means forty trains an hour, during the midday period, from the De Kalb Avenue station to Manhattan via both Montague Street Tunnel and the Manhattan Bridge.

Service on the Prospect Park Queensboro Plaza line will be doubled, in conjunction with the Brighton line midday service. Trains will operate every three and three-quarter minutes.

MOTHER TRIES TO DROWN BABE AND THEN KILL SELF

A nervous disorder, brought on by the birth of a baby two months ago, caused Mrs. Gertrude Provisor, twenty-six, 931 Main Avenue, Passaic, N. J., to become despondent yesterday, and she attempted to drown her infant daughter, Eleanor, in a bathtub.

When the child, long submerged, no longer struggled, Mrs. Provisor picked up a bread knife and then tried to end her own life by slashing her left wrist and her throat.

That the pretty mother and the infant were still alive last night was due to the fact that another daughter, Ruth, five, became hungry about that time. Mrs. Provisor's husband, Meyer, is proprietor of a drug store in the building where the Provisofs live.

"Go upstairs to mother and she will fix you something," Mr. Provisor said. The girl ran upstairs and searched through the apartment for her mother. Finally, in the bathroom, to a pool of blood, she found her mother. In the bathtub Ruth saw the unconscious form of her baby sister.

Screaming, Ruth rushed back to her father and told him the horrible sight she had seen. Mr. Provisor rushed upstairs, where he found his wife unconscious. He immediately took the infant from the bathtub, and after working frantically for several minutes succeeded in reviving the baby.

After receiving emergency treatment administered by Dr. Abraham Machlin, Mrs. Provisor was removed to St. Mary's Hospital in a serious condition.

Mr. Provisor said his wife had been very nervous since the birth of little Eleanor. Eleanor, he said, has a good chance to recover, but the mother's chances to live are slight.

Woman Poisoned From Gas

Mary Quirk, ninety-two, of 428 De Kalb Avenue, Brooklyn, was taken to Cumberland Street Hospital yesterday suffering from gas poisoning.

FOREIGN NEWS

Wedding Bells for Kaiser.
Princess Must Die.
Another War.
And Another Assassination.

Princess Hermine

BERLIN.— William Hohenzollern, former Kaiser, flatly refuses to break his engagement to Princess Hermine, pretty widow, whom he is to marry November 5. Word was received here that the party of men archists, who went to Doorn to protest against the proposed marriage, had been informed by the Kaiser that the marriage would take place as scheduled. The German delegation discussed the financial status of the Hohenzollerns, particularly the allowance of the Crown Princess, who is bitterly opposed to the marriage.

MOSCOW. — Princess Anna Troubeskaya, daughter of a Kiev professor, has been sentenced to death by a Soviet tribunal. She was arrested at Vladivostok and charged with being a spy in the service of the Japanese Government.

BUCHAREST. — The Russian Soviet has seized upon the arrest of two Russian aviators who crashed to earth at Bessarabia four months ago as a pretext to precipitate war with Rumania, Government officials here claim.

PARIS. — An Eastern telegraph agency dispatch from Moscow states there was an unconfirmed report that Minister of the Interior Djerdjinski of the Soviet Government had been assassinated.

BERLIN.—The German Foreign Office issued an official denial of reports from foreign capitals that Germany had made or was contemplating an alliance with Russia and Turkey.

LONDON.—A rumor that a British battleship had met disaster in the Dardanelles is officially denied here.

MOSCOW. — Leon Trotsky is busily engaged with the reorganization of the Russian fleet, according to reports here.

Don't Miss These Features in Today's SUNDAY NEWS.

Real love stories with happy endings—our readers tell them. —Page 16.

Are you following the amazing adventures of Prince Charming in "An Heir at Large"? —Page 33.

A study of eyebrows among the Upper Four Hundred.—Page 27.

Perry Winkle and Chester Gump make things hum. Two full-page cartoons. —Pages 28 and 29.

Movie magic silhouetted in a page of delightful pictures of latest offerings.—Page 24.

Reno's divorce colony under the microscope as seen by Judge Bartlett, famous divorce judge. —Page 16.

Charming patterns for garments to be worn at home. —Page 34.

Guy Lee slams New York wise in a vicious poem.—Page 31.

Red asks Ira Riddle for tour in "The..."

The real babe of the Ruth family. Note how much she looks like mother.

(C) 1922: The SUNDAY NEWS: N.Y.

2

The Babe's Babe

The New York Yankees were in Cleveland on September 23, 1922, closing in on a second consecutive American League pennant, when it was revealed via front page headlines that Babe Ruth was a father.

The circumstances surrounding the discovery were truly sensational. The headline in the *New York American* read, "Ruth A Daddy For Sixteen Months And Has Hidden Facts From World," while the *New York Daily News* was equally shocked: "The Secret Is Out! Babe Ruth Has A Baby Sixteen Months Old!"

That baby was me. In a matter of hours, I went from relative obscurity to being the most celebrated child in New York City. The way people were making a fuss, you would think *I* was the one hitting all those home runs. I guess that when you're Babe Ruth's babe, being the center of attention comes with the territory.

The consensus was that I resembled my father the most. Helen Ruth, my father's wife of eight years, was often heard to remark, "Don't you think Dorothy is the dead image of her father? Her nose is the duplicate of my husband's. See how it turns up." The newspapers ran pictures of Helen, Babe and myself together, enabling people to make their own determinations.

Everyone's first reaction was "Cute baby, but where's she been for the past sixteen months?" Somehow my father had kept me a secret from a New York press that rarely let him out of its sight. The distinguished members of the media were astounded to learn of my father's indoctrination into parenthood and intended to find out the details.

When reporters confronted him in Cleveland, he acted as if nothing out of the ordinary had taken place. "Oh, you found out about that," he nonchalantly replied as he searched for his bat. "Yep, Dorothy's getting to be a big girl now. She weighed only two pounds when she came into the world, and for a while we weren't sure if the rascal would live.

"But when we put her in an incubator, she began to pick up right away, and now she's just as healthy as any other kid. It just happens that nothing was said in the newspapers at the time, and neither Mrs. Ruth or myself made any effort to have it generally known."

Meanwhile, at the Ansonia Hotel on Broadway and 73rd Street back in New York, Helen was also being interrogated. Annoyed by the intrusion into her privacy, Helen acted defensively when asked if the baby was adopted. "Adopted?" she barked. "I should say not. That baby's mine, mine, *mine!*" She became so enraged that she refused to allow the photographers to take pictures of the two of us.

Eventually she calmed down enough to explain that I had been born with rickets, a disease caused by vitamin D deficiency and characterized by a softening of the bones; because of this, a nurse had cared for me for the first fourteen months of my life. I weighed only two pounds at birth, and remained extremely underweight and frail for the first three or four years of my life. After I became healthy enough to live without the aid of an incubator, Helen continued, she and Babe had brought me to live with them at the Ansonia Hotel. She refused to identify the name of the nurse who had cared for me, and, by way of explanation for keeping me a secret, told the reporters that my father had feared being ridiculed by his friends and teammates because of how small and sickly I was.

Two months earlier, clerks in the Ansonia Hotel recalled seeing Helen pushing a baby carriage, never realizing that the baby was her own but figuring instead that she was babysitting for a friend. When some of the clerks were questioned by reporters, they smiled and admitted that my father used to sneak around the hotel cradling a baby in his arms. The clerks of course were suspicious, but they never confronted Babe or Helen because it was simply none of their business. One clerk volunteered, "Mrs. Ruth would take the baby for a walk around four o'clock and be joined by Babe around seven o'clock, when he returned from the ballpark." Another clerk said, "Sometimes Babe would come down the stairs, bouncing the baby on his shoulder."

Still, the mystery was coming no closer to being solved. Babe told newspapermen in Cleveland that I was born on February 2, 1921, in Presbyterian Hospital on 168th Street and Riverside Drive, while Helen said I was born on June 7, 1921, in St. Vincent's Hospital on Seventh Avenue in Greenwich Village. Helen explained the contradiction: "Babe was born on February 2, and obviously confused the child's birthday with his own." She gave no explanation for why he had forgotten which hospital.

Further investigation revealed that St. Vincent's was not a maternity hospital, nor was there any record of my birth at the Bureau of Vital Statistics. Adding to the mystery, the Department of Health, where physicians were legally required to record all births, also provided no record of my birth in 1920, 1921 or 1922.

On top of all that, Helen said I was christened in a Roman Catholic church on 68th Street. St. Catherine's was the only Roman Catholic church on 68th Street, and the priest in charge of christenings, Father Sullivan, had no recollection of christening a girl named Dorothy Helen Ruth. "The daughter of Babe Ruth?" remarked Father Sullivan. "Oh, I'd remember christening *his* baby."

A few days later, while everyone frantically tried to put the pieces of this bizarre puzzle together, Helen spent a restful day with a reporter from the *New York Daily News* in her room at the Ansonia. Up until this point, it had not been common knowledge that she and Babe had ever had any children, so it came as a shock to most people when they read the next day in the *Daily News* that Helen had reflected somberly on the untimely deaths of their three previous children.

"The first one was Helen," said Mrs. Ruth, as she slowly ran her finger the length of the child's picture on the mantlepiece. "She died when she was only a few days old. The fat baby was George Jr.," she continued. "He was taken away when he was only four months old. And Margaret left us when she was only one and a half." She failed to elaborate, and since the births and subsequent deaths had been such well-kept secrets, no details exist to this day.

Helen explained how fond Babe was of me, so much so that he used to call me every night, no matter where he was playing. "Babe thinks the world of Dorothy," she told the reporter. "I'm not allowed to go to any of the games unless I bring Dorothy with me."

Within a few days of her interview, Helen was again being badgered with the same adoption questions. The press was well aware that she had a history of emotional instability, and it was being severely tested. "I told you that baby is rightfully mine!" she screamed. "I told you, she had to be cared for by a nurse for fourteen months, it was necessary to keep her birth a secret." Finally, she refused to answer any more questions. She had grown so confused, it's possible that by this point she might not have known what the truth was.

Around this time, my father called Helen and told her to come to Boston for the Yankees' series with the Red Sox, and on September 26 a limousine pulled away from the Ansonia carrying the two of us to the train station.

In Boston Babe paraded around the field, introducing me to his teammates as the official mascot of the Yankees. With

Babe and Helen together for the first time since the story broke, the media swarmed all over them, backing them into the corner of the dugout. Many of the reporters had spent the last three days chasing phantom leads, and they were in no mood to be lied to anymore. They wanted—and expected—nothing less than the truth. And to say they were skeptical of my origin was an understatement.

Babe attempted to resolve all the confusion: "It's all very simple, this mystery bunk. Why, I can't even remember the names of towns I've just left, I travel around so much.

"And I have the same lapse of memory about the names of hospitals. We didn't make public the arrival of the baby until recently, because she had been very sick. We fought hard to save her life," he desperately exclaimed. "For months, Helen had been tied down, watching the cradle. Anyway, whatever my wife says goes with me."

Not missing a beat, Helen grabbed me from Babe's arms: "Little Dorothy is my baby and I ought to know. Goodness knows I went through enough anxiety trying to save her little life. And of course our close friends knew all about it. It just didn't happen to get into the newspapers, and we were glad for once that our personal affairs escaped the normal publicity."

The reporters continued to shoot holes in her story, reiterating the same question they had asked her last week: "Where has Dorothy been for the past sixteen months?"

Helen was growing frustrated because she did not have a more believable story. One reporter said, "We can clear all of this up if you'll just tell us the name of the hospital. We've already checked St. Vincent's—"

Incensed, Helen interrupted, "She was not born in St. Vincent's Hospital! I'm not going to tell you where she was born!

"People have been very mean about making all this mystery about Dorothy," she went on. "I won't give them the satisfaction of telling them anything."

My father joined in, growling, "I suppose we should have sent out invitations to all the fans to come and call on the princess, and because we didn't there's a mystery someplace."

That was that. The impromptu press conference was over. Babe and Helen adamantly refused to discuss the matter further. As they turned and walked away, reporters could only scratch their heads in disbelief.

A teammate of my father's, third baseman Joe Dugan, once said, "Babe Ruth wasn't born, he fell out of a tree." Well, it must have looked like I had fallen out of that same tree!

3

Breaking the Rules

Although my arrival on the scene in September of 1922 stirred up quite a bit of controversy, it paled in comparison to the rest of Babe's year, unquestionably his most frustrating year in baseball. Not only was he suspended five times, he was also fined, thrown out of three games and removed as captain of the Yankees.

My father had made plans to embark on his traditional barnstorming tour around the country, this time accompanied by teammate Bob Meusel, two young Yankee pitchers, and a collection of semipro players from New York. The team was called the Babe Ruth All-Stars, and they were scheduled to tour for about two weeks, with stops in Jamestown and Elmira, New York, Scranton, Pennsylvania, and Oklahoma City, Oklahoma, among other places. Babe enjoyed these barnstorming tours almost as much as playing during the regular season; traveling around the country gave him an opportunity to entertain people in small towns, folks who otherwise would never get a chance to see him play.

But there was another, more important reason why he wanted to keep up the practice of going on the tours: Dad often made anywhere from $15,000 to $30,000 for these exhibitions, which was usually more money than he got paid for an entire season. For this particular tour he figured to earn $25,000, an astonishing sum of money for two weeks' work.

When barnstorming first became popular in the early 1900s, fans were given a special treat: Not only did they get to witness competitive baseball, they also were provided with the opportunity to meet their favorite stars. Over time, however, the tours began to consist of only a couple of stars from each team; the rest were amateurs and semipro players. So what the fans were really getting for their money was a team of imposters who billed themselves as World Series heroes.

The owners came to the rescue in 1911, instituting a law which prohibited any World Series participants from playing in exhibition games after their performances in the World Series. Dad and a few of his teammates with the Red Sox ignored this rule in 1916, when they played a series of exhibitions throughout New England, and were fined for it. But my father always felt that certain rules did not apply to him.

Judge Kenesaw Mountain Landis, the newly elected baseball commissioner, warned Babe that if he went ahead with his plans, the consequences would be severe. Landis's uncompromising reputation was well known, even though he was just nearing the end of his first full year on the job, and Babe was well aware that he was challenging the authority of the wrong man. Still, he figured that the worst that could possibly happen would be that he would have to pay a stiff fine: in all likelihood $3,362, his share for playing on the losing team in the World Series. Since he had estimated making about eight times that amount on his tour, he could well afford to forfeit three or four thousand. Therefore, when Dad was informed of the commissioner's position, he responded, "Tell the old guy to jump in the lake." (In fact, in Jamestown, one of his first stops on the tour, Babe hit a home run into Lake Chautauqua—it has yet to be retrieved.)

Shortly after Babe left on the tour, Landis ruled that both Babe and Bob Meusel were to forfeit their entire World Series shares, just as Babe had suspected. But Landis was true to his reputation—both men in addition were suspended for the first six weeks of the 1922 season. Babe was apologetic and intended to plea bargain when he visited Landis in his hotel suite in New Orleans shortly before the season began, but Judge Landis's court was not an appeals court, and all Babe got for his efforts was a lengthy lecture on respect for authority and discipline.

After a six-week exile from the game, Babe returned to action on May 20 against the St. Louis Browns. My father was understandably rusty, striking out in his first at-bat and failing to get the ball out of the infield in his next three.

Dad amused the fans the next day when he came to bat in the first inning waving an emerald beauty—that's right, a shiny Irish-green bat. Admirers in Baltimore, his home town, had sent the bat as a present. I never knew Dad to be that superstitious, but I guess he was willing to try anything to change his luck.

In his first two at-bats he popped out weakly to the infield. Nevertheless, Babe had a way of giving the fans their money's worth, even when he did not hit a home run. Each time he walked back to the dugout, he joked with the fans, who rolled in the aisles at his antics. Finally, in the eighth inning, Dad found his pot of gold at the end of the rainbow when he smashed his first home run of the 1922 season— the last time Babe used that bat.

His problems continued the following day, as he left the bases loaded three times. A crowd of 38,000, the largest of the year at the Polo Grounds, booed his futile attempts. Babe was not accustomed to getting booed, especially in his home park. On May 24, in a game against the Washington Senators, his frustration finally got the best of him. Late in the game, Babe singled to Sam Rice in center field and tried to stretch it into a double. The play was close, but umpire George Hildebrand called my father out. Babe became enraged; he grabbed a handful of dirt and threw it at Hildebrand—in his face, as it appeared to the crowd and was subsequently reported in the newspapers.

On his way to the bench Babe tipped his cap and bowed to the fans, many of whom were razzing him because of his poor performance. One particular fan, who was cursing him incessantly, infuriated him so much that he jumped onto the dugout and chased the poor fellow through the stands. It was a good thing for my father that the fan escaped—and a good thing for the fan!

When American League President Ban Johnson received word of the incident, he assumed that there were extenuating circumstances and reacted sympathetically. "The hero of a year ago was ridden by the fans and at times abused," Johnson told the press. "Ruth plainly did not possess the mental strength and stability to brave this sudden reversal of public adoration.

"For this offense, Ruth is fined $200 and removed from captaincy of the club. It is my opinion that his present mental temperament disqualifies him for the position."

Babe was grateful for the president's lenience, since he realized that he easily could have been suspended again. "I'm sorry it happened, but I stood as much as I could and I had to break loose," he stated.

He went on to explain his actions: "They can boo and hoot me all they want. That doesn't matter to me. But when a fan calls insulting names from the grandstand and becomes abusive, I don't intend to stand for it. That fellow in New York last Thursday, whoever he was, called me a 'low-down bum' and other names that got me mad, and when I ran after him, he ran.

"Furthermore, I didn't throw any dirt in Hildebrand's face. It didn't go into his face, only on his sleeve. I don't see why I should get any punishment at all. I would go into the stands again if I had to."

On June 19, with the Yankees mired in an eight-game

losing streak, Babe was thrown out again for arguing another close play at second base. Umpire Bill Dinneen tossed Babe out of the game for what he termed "vulgar abuse." The following day, in response to his actions, Ban Johnson suspended Babe for three days. Babe was furious and foolishly went looking for Dinneen, hoping to even the score—with physical violence, if necessary. After a series of harsh words between the two, Cleveland Indians first baseman Stuffy McInnis intervened before any blows were landed. Dinneen filed another report with the American League office, and Babe's suspension was increased to five days.

By the end of the season, my father had played in only 110 games out of a possible 154, been suspended five times, and engaged in a fight with teammate Wally Pipp where Dad failed to land one punch. His statistics were even more depressing: 35 home runs, 24 less than he had hit the previous season, and 72 fewer RBIs, one of only two times in his career as a full-time player that he failed to garner 100. Worst of all, many critics were finally convinced that pitchers had found Babe's weakness at the plate, and that his phenomenal success in 1920 and 1921 would never be duplicated. The final insult came in the World Series against the Giants, in which he hit an abysmal .118 in a losing cause.

Babe's disastrous season proved that he was human. Though baseball came naturally to him, he realized that he was going to have to work harder and concentrate if he wanted to regain his top form. He had allowed himself to be distracted by commercial endorsements, petty squabbles with team officials, broken curfews and a host of other errors in judgment. He thought he owned New York City and that the party would never end. It was one of the only times in his career that his popularity went to his head, but New York City was just the city to teach him a much-needed lesson in humility.

Three weeks after the Series, some of the sportswriters who covered the Yankees organized a dinner in Babe's honor—or so they led Babe to believe. The evening at the Elks Club in Manhattan turned out to be anything but a lighthearted "roast."

After many of Babe's friends had taken turns lambasting him, New York state senator James Walker, the future mayor of New York, unfurled an unexpected, vitriolic verbal assault. Walker criticized Babe for letting down the fans of New York, his teammates, his friends, himself, and, most importantly, the "dirty-faced kids" of America who idolized him.

My father was reduced to tears. Walker's speech affected him more than any of the fights, suspensions or statistical failures of the past year. When he could finally respond, he said, "I know as well as anybody else just what mistakes I made last season. There's no use in me trying to get away from them.

"But let me tell you something. I want the New York fans and sportswriters to know that I've had my last drink until next October. I mean it. Tomorrow I'm going to my farm. I'm going to work my head off—and maybe part of my stomach." When I think of important turning points in his career, that night belongs at the top. From that moment on, Dad really had something to prove.

With the events of a tumultuous season behind him, Babe left for his farm in Sudbury, Massachusetts, with Helen and I in tow. He intended to lick his wounds, stick to a regimented diet, and work himself back into shape.

Babe and Helen had purchased "Home Plate Farm" in 1916, while my father was still playing with the Boston Red Sox; life in the country was a welcome change of pace from the distractions and temptations of big-city living. The eighty-acre farm was located about twenty miles outside of Boston, next to the estate of automobile tycoon Henry Ford. The sunny, cheerful two-story colonial had three bedrooms, servants' quarters and a bathroom upstairs, and a living room and big country kitchen downstairs.

My father's daily activities enabled him to get a much-needed headstart on spring training. When he wasn't hunting, fishing or horseback riding, he was remodeling the farmhouse, chopping wood and raising chickens, turkeys and White English pit bulls. I never knew why I was forbidden to go near the barn until one day seventy-five pit bulls escaped from their pen, which was inside, and killed a herd of cows on the Ford estate. Not only did my father have to pay for the cows, he also had to shoot all the dogs because once they get the taste of blood, they become too dangerous to handle.

Dad's commitment to excellence paid huge dividends in 1923. He stayed out of manager Miller Huggins's doghouse and went on to win his only Most Valuable Player Award; his .393 batting average and 205 hits were both career highs, while his home run total of 41 was good enough to lead the league, though modest compared to his totals in 1920 and 1921.

With Babe at the top of his game, the Yankees won their third successive pennant and their first World Championship, beating their cross-town rivals, the New York Giants, in six games. Dad hit three home runs, scored eight runs and batted .368 as the Yankees finally disposed of the Giants after being embarrassed by them the previous two years. The year 1923 was vintage Babe Ruth.

Meanwhile, Helen and I spent almost four blissful years on the farm, from 1920 to 1924, with Babe visiting whenever he could get away from his commitments in the city. Summers were spent riding horses and going on picnics, while winters were devoted to building snowmen, sleigh-riding, and sitting in front of the fireplace and drinking hot chocolate. In the fall, the three of us took long walks in the woods to admire the foliage, and Dad would usually carry me on his shoulders.

But the good times that we shared together as a family were about to come to an end. Babe and Helen's marriage had been on the rocks for quite some time, and the prospects of a reconciliation seemed remote. Looking back at the years they spent together, their separation in 1925 seemed inevitable from the start.

In 1914, when my father met sixteen-year-old Helen Woodford, a waitress in Lander's coffeeshop in Boston, he immediately fell in love with her. After a courtship of less than four months, the two eloped, marrying in St. Paul's Catholic Church in Ellicott City, Maryland, on October 17, 1914.

Helen was introverted, naive and totally unaware of the life she would lead married to a baseball player. And my father was to be no ordinary baseball player. His career was in its fledgling stage with the Boston Red Sox, and neither Helen nor anyone else possibly could have foreseen the sequence of events that would catapult him into the national spotlight.

Part of their first year together was spent in a small apartment in Baltimore. Babe had been anxious to get married and uncharacteristically enjoyed being domesticated, but he had yet to experience life as a major-league star. Money, women, booze, weeks away from home, and the nightlife of a big city like Boston all began to compete with his marriage.

The Red Sox won the World Series in 1915, 1916 and again in 1918, and Dad was the most talked-about pitcher in baseball. As his celebrity increased, he enjoyed his freedom more and more. Helen, on the other hand, wanted no part of his lavish new lifestyle, which did not seem to bother Babe in the slightest; he was spending money faster than he could earn it, and having the time of his life without her.

Helen managed to cope with the loneliness, but the rumors of Babe's infidelities crushed her. It got to the point where Dad would completely ignore Helen when she confronted him about his extracurricular activities with women. His indifference towards her caused Helen the most pain and eventually led to her drinking and pill-taking. Frequently she had to be hospitalized because of nervous breakdowns. She became so distraught while visiting my father in the hospital on one occasion that she had to remain there as a patient after he was released.

Babe and Helen's move to New York City in 1920 simply exacerbated the situation, providing more temptations for

Babe and more frustrations for Helen. Helen and I would come down from Boston to stay with Babe when the Yankees were playing at home, but when the Yankees went on the road, we returned to Sudbury. The constant shuttling between New York and Boston slowly wore her out.

To make matters worse, my father's relationships with other women were becoming harder to ignore. Babe denied the rumors, but the truth was in the papers. The name most often mentioned in connection with his was Claire Merritt Hodgson. Claire was an attractive young widow from Athens, Georgia, who had previously dated Ty Cobb, the famous ballplayer of the Detroit Tigers. Babe insisted that "they were just good friends," but half of New York knew otherwise because he spent more time at her apartment on 79th Street than at his own.

Just before Claire was fifteen years old she dropped out of school and ran off with Frank Hodgson, a widower more than twice her age, to whom she referred as "the catch of the town." He was a wealthy businessman from Atlanta, and his relatives were influential cotton brokers. Even the birth of Julia, a year and a half after they were married, could not save their ill-fated marriage. Shortly thereafter, Claire separated from her husband and, without telling her parents, left for New York City with Julia and her twenty-year-old maid, Marie Martin, in November of 1920.

Apprehensive but determined, Claire went directly to the Waldorf Astoria Hotel—the only hotel she had ever heard of. During her first few years in New York, she earned a steady income as a model, posing for some of the most famous artists of the day: Howard Chandler Christie, Harrison Fisher and Penrhyn Stanlaws, to name a few. Later she danced with the Ziegfeld Follies and appeared on stage in *The Magic Melody*. Her acting talents were mediocre, but her physical appearance was striking.

In 1922 Claire received word that Frank Hodgson had died, and her family begged her to return to Athens, Georgia, so that they could help ease the burden of raising a child on her own. But Claire had grown accustomed to her new surroundings and realized that her future was in New York, not Athens. When her father died the following year, Claire's two brothers, Hubert and Eugene, and her mother, Carrie Merritt, agreed to move to New York to live with her.

James Barton, a good friend of Babe's, introduced Claire to my father at a ballgame in Washington in 1923. Their relationship quickly developed, and before long the pair were hot talk for the gossip columns, although they were as discreet as possible, usually eating dinner in the apartment. Claire was so overly cautious, in fact, that she would not even hang a picture of my father in her apartment because she was afraid a neighbor or a delivery boy might become suspicious. They became so close that Claire even accompanied Babe on his visits to Helen in Sudbury, checking into a hotel in downtown Boston and waiting for him to return. I heard about all this years later, from my father's teammates.

At the end of 1924 Helen had decided that she had had enough. She packed her belongings, told my father she was taking me with her, and left on a train for Boston. Only this time she wasn't returning.

At the same time, Claire desperately wanted to marry my father and pressured him constantly. Babe remained steadfast in his beliefs. "I'm a Catholic and she's a Catholic, and we can't get a divorce," he repeatedly told her. "It's against my religion."

On August 4, 1925, after living apart for seven months, Babe and Helen legally separated on account of incompatibility. As part of the separation agreement, Helen was awarded the astounding sum of $100,000, to be paid in four installments: the first in October 1925 and the last in October 1928. Furthermore, I was placed in Helen's custody, all of this as I approached my fifth birthday.

4

Helen Help Me

Now that she and my father were separated, Helen undertook the difficult task of raising a daughter and running a large farm singlehandedly. Even though it was not a working farm, the substantial piece of land had to be maintained. It proved to be an impossible task for a woman whose health was constantly failing and who was incapable of handling pressure.

Helen was forced to rely upon Fanny Bailey, who my father had hired at my birth to take care of me. Fanny was a large, heavyset black woman in her early thirties. When she gave me a hug, I would totally disappear into the folds of her arms—those were major league hugs! Fanny once told me that I was so small at birth, she could hold me in the palm of her hand. When she took me out for a walk, I was so scrawny and frail-looking that she covered the baby carriage with a veil.

As a child, some of my happiest moments were spent with Fanny. She would put my highchair in front of the woodburning stove, and we would sing songs together, like "My Blue Heaven." It seemed as if I learned how to sing that song before I even learned how to talk! As I got older, I would help her prepare meals by washing the vegetables. For a while I even thought that Fanny was my mother, especially because Helen spent so much time in hospitals. One day, when she heard me call Fanny "Mommy," she became very upset and immediately put an end to that.

Life in Sudbury came to an end in 1926, when Helen had finally had enough and decided to sell the farm. Helen, Fanny and I, a curious trio if ever there was one, packed our bags and moved to Watertown, a large, suburban town a few miles west of Boston.

It wasn't long before Helen found a new boyfriend, Dr. Edward H. Kinder, a handsome, well-known local dentist. As far as I was concerned, he was just a friend who was staying with us. I accepted him because Helen did not push him on me and never introduced him as my new father. Dr. Kinder was very quiet and not the type who would ever bounce me on his knee—quite the opposite of my father. With the proceeds from the sale of the Sudbury farm, Helen helped Dr. Kinder finance the construction of a new home, on Quincy Street in Watertown, and in May of 1927 the three of us moved in—or, rather the two of them moved in: Helen had decided to send me away to the School of the Assumption, a convent school in Wellesley Hills. Boarding school was to become my permanent address, all of this at the ripe old age of seven.

I was frightened when I first arrived at Assumption, but Helen assured me that time would pass quickly, and that she would come visit me on weekends. Six months went by like six years; Helen never came to visit me, and boarding school was worse than I ever imagined. Babe never visited, either. I remember lying awake at night and thinking that my father and Helen must have died, and no one had had the decency to tell me. I was extremely intimidated by the thought of making friends because I had rarely been around children my own age, so I was content to spend most of the day cooped up in my room. I felt like a recluse.

Weekends were spent alone at the school, while all the other kids went home to the love and attention of their families. I never gave up hope that my father or Helen would come and visit me, but they never did. I felt as if no one even knew I was alive. At night I remember crying so hard that the nuns in my dormitory had someone sleep in my room with me. When that didn't work, they simply told me to shut up because I was keeping everyone awake.

I couldn't wait until the Thanksgiving and Christmas holidays because I would get to see Fanny—until I learned that Helen had dismissed her, with the reason that her services were no longer needed now that I was in boarding school. If I had felt lonely before, now I felt totally abandoned. (Fanny and I did not meet again until fifteen years later, when I was twenty-two. I asked her if she would help me take care of my second child, Genevieve, who was ill at the time, and she agreed. We spent a very happy six months together.)

I had yet to reach my eighth birthday, but I already felt like I had had enough of life. Little did I know, however, that life was just beginning.

On Friday night, January 11, 1929, a mysterious fire broke out in the home of Helen and Dr. Kinder. A neighbor saw smoke coming from the ground-floor windows around 10:00 P.M. and immediately called the fire department. Helen was home alone in the house that night. The police later determined that she had been sitting in an easy chair to the left of the bed when the fire started; she was dressed in her nightgown and had bed linens wrapped around her, so most likely she had fallen asleep in the chair and was overcome by smoke and hence unable to make it to safety. Because of the dense smoke, Captain John Kelley of the Watertown Fire Department had to crawl on his hands and knees to reach Helen's bedroom on the second floor. As Kelley blindly felt his way into the room, he accidentally brushed against Helen's body, which was lying face down, about ten feet from the door. She was still breathing.

Along with another fireman, Kelley carried Helen's inert form downstairs and across the street to a neighbor's house, where the firefighters tried unsuccessfully to revive her. Helen died minutes before a doctor was able to reach her.

Since the neighbors knew that "the Kinders" had a little girl, it was feared that I might still be in the house, so another fireman reentered the burning building. He retrieved a badly-burned, life-sized doll, which for a moment he had thought might be me.

Dr. Kinder was watching a boxing match at the Boston Garden when he was notified of the fire. He returned home immediately with no idea of the full extent of the tragedy until the police met him at the front door and explained what had happened. He went to pieces at the news, unable to believe that Helen was dead. And how was he going to explain to the police that Helen Kinder was really Helen Ruth?

He wasn't. The police were informed that the dead woman was Helen Kinder, his wife. Fearing that further questions might ruin his reputation and hoping to avoid a scandal, Dr. Kinder disappeared from public view, going into hiding at his parents' house in Boston.

No one had any reason to doubt his story, including the neighbors, who confirmed the fact that Dr. and Mrs. Kinder had been living quietly with their young daughter at 47 Quincy Street for about two years. The name on the death certificate, signed by medical examiner George West, was Helen Kinder. The cause of death was listed as "suffocation and incineration."

Saturday morning, while funeral arrangements were being made, the police department began to receive telephone calls from people who had seen Helen's photograph in the newspaper and identified her as Babe Ruth's wife. The masquerade was over. The funeral was postponed while everyone searched for the "mystery man," Dr. Kinder, who was nowhere to be found.

Because of all the confusion, my father was not notified of Helen's death until late Saturday evening, more than twenty-four hours after her death. He was understandably shaken when he received the news and insisted on taking the next available train to Boston to help with the funeral arrangements.

When he arrived at the train station in Boston early Sunday morning, he was greeted by an old friend from his Red Sox days, Arthur Crowley, son of the Boston Police Superintendent, Michael Crowley. The first words out of my father's mouth were "Where's my little girl? I've got to see her." Crowley assured Babe that I was safe in the School of the Assumption.

Instead of going directly to Watertown, the two men drove to the Brunswick Hotel in Boston so that my father could rest for a few hours and collect his thoughts before reading a prepared statement to the press.

"My wife and I have not lived together for the past three years," the statement began. "During that time I have seldom seen her. I've done all that I can to comply with her wishes. Her death is a great shock. That is all I wish to say."

The reporters had many questions, but my father was as much in the dark as they were and could not provide any more concrete answers. "There is plenty to talk about, but I am not going to say anything while Mrs. Ruth's body is above ground," he said. "I may have something for the critics later." This less than satisfied the reporters, but they could see how much my father had suffered and thus respected his privacy.

Meanwhile, Helen's relatives, most of whom lived in the Boston area, had gotten wind of Helen's new "Mrs. Kinder" identity and were outraged. They demanded to know what really happened to Helen, suspecting foul play and insisting on a full-scale police investigation. The fact that Helen and Dr. Kinder were not married became a minor issue compared to the new allegations and accusations which were brought forth. Mrs. William Woodford, Helen's mother, accused, "Helen never died by accident; she was done to death." One of her brothers insisted, "Helen told me she knew a doctor who would give her opium tablets."

Another brother, William Woodford, an ex-police officer, was the most outspoken of all. He told Middlesex County District Attorney Robert Bushnell he believed that the fire was intentionally started, and that Helen was drugged so she would not be able to escape. "What is there to prove that the house was not fired?" he demanded. "What is there to prove that she was not murdered?"

These new developments convinced the district attorney that federal narcotics agents should be called in to investigate Kinder's possible involvement in illegal drug use. Meanwhile, Bushnell, not wanting to be second-guessed, ordered the body to be taken to the medical examiner for an autopsy. Complications arose because the body had already been embalmed, so the contents of Helen's stomach could not be properly analyzed. "The embalming fluid used by the undertaker has caused the stomach contents to coagulate," Dr. West stated to the press. "In such cases, odors are lost, and it is impossible to determine just what the contents of the stomach are."

On Monday afternoon Dr. Kinder unexpectedly walked into the police station in Watertown, intent on setting the record straight and clearing himself of any accusations of wrongdoing. He told police that he had invited Helen to go with him to the fights on Friday night, but she had said that she did not feel well and wished to remain home. He also said he did not recall telling police that Mrs. Ruth was Mrs. Kinder, but did agree that it was possible, during all of the commotion, for him to have grown confused. He then blamed Helen for any misunderstanding concering their marital status, saying, "The neighbors and members of my family who believed we were married did so because Helen told them we were." Kinder's family believed that he and Helen were married in Montreal in 1927, but he assured the police that at no time was he married to Helen and that "we were just good friends."

"I never married her, but I lived with her for two years, and I've done nothing morally wrong," Dr. Kinder said. He went on to tell Police Chief John Millmore that he was friendly with Babe Ruth, and the slugger knew that Helen and he were living together.

After three hours of questioning, Kinder was exonerated. "I'm satisfied," said Police Chief Millmore, "that Kinder had no connection with the fire or death of Mrs. Ruth."

Kinder was only telling part of the truth. Police later found canceled checks proving that Helen used part of Babe's separation money to help pay for the Kinder house on Quincy Street and maintain their comfortable lifestyle—odd behavior for just a good friend. Kinder's relatives admitted that *he* had told them that Helen and he had married in Montreal, and they were listed in the Watertown telephone directory as husband and wife. But the federal narcotic agents who checked into Kinder's affairs never found any proof that he was involved in illegal drugs.

There was some deception on Babe's part as well. When he was informed of Kinder's statements concerning their friendship, he denied ever meeting him or having any knowledge of Helen living with him. Yet Babe would visit Helen whenever the Yankees played the Red Sox in Boston, which was quite frequently.

The details of the case did not reach New York until Monday, but when they did, the newspapers couldn't find headlines big enough to print the story. The *New York Evening Post* screamed, "Mrs. Ruth's Family Charges 'Foul Play' In Death In Fire." The *New York Daily News* was equally sensational: Babe Ruth's Wife Dies In Fire At Secret Love-Life Bungalow." And the *New York American*, always ready with a juicy headline, bellowed, "Mrs. Babe Ruth Dies In Fire; Her Secret Romance Bared."

Back in Boston, the consensus among the authorities was that Helen's death was purely accidental, and that the case should be closed. Most people were in agreement, but William Woodford was not. With William's vivid imagination fueling the fire, his nineteen-year-old sister Nora told reporters: "Almost four weeks ago, Helen asked me to accompany her to New York, because Babe wanted a divorce so he could marry Claire Hodgson."

Nora recalled the exchange which took place on December 10 between Babe and Helen in the New York law offices of Christy Walsh, Babe's personal friend and financial advisor of nine years. "All right. I'll go to Reno and get a divorce quietly so your reputation in baseball won't be ruined, but you've got to pay my expenses out there and give me $100,000," Helen offered.

Babe responded with "Go to hell. I've already given you enough money."

The Woodfords' comments convinced the district attorney that a further investigation was necessary. Bushnell, against his better judgment, ordered a second autopsy, this time to be performed by medical examiner George B. MacGrath, who was from another district and whose equipment was better suited to analyze the contents of the stomach. He concurred with Dr. West: "There was no evidence of alcohol, drugs or 'foul play'." The district attorney concluded, "There was no murder in this case. Death was caused by burning."

Chief John W. O'Hearn of the Watertown Fire Department attributed the fire to "defective wiring and overloading of wires." His report was confirmed by Ellis Dennis, the state examiner of electricians: "A most thorough investigation was made, and there is no doubt that the cause of the fire was the overloading of the electrical system. Fuse plugs were found in use up to thirty amps where they should not have been over ten, and when a short circuit occurred, these plugs held the resistance, heating the wires and starting the fire."

The Woodford family was at last satisfied with these reports and the case was closed. Helen's burial could finally take place.

On Thursday morning, January 17, less than one week after she had died, Helen was buried in Old Calvary Cemetery in Boston, following a brief funeral service in the Woodford home.

Maybe no one will ever know what really happened the night of January 11, 1929. A thorough investigation *was* performed, convincing the authorities that Helen's death was unquestionably accidental, but there was one potential lead at least that was never followed up. At the bottom of a news story, it was reported that a Watertown policeman had seen an automobile driving away from the front of the Kinder home, where it had been parked suspiciously for some time, five minutes before the house burst into flames.

I remained in the School of the Assumption, unvisited and unaware of Helen's death and the legal fight over my custody which was developing between Babe and Helen's sister, Johanna Woodford McCarthy. Johanna was threatening to take Babe to court to prevent him from bringing me to New York to live with him. She did not feel he was entitled to guardianship.

"I want her for my own," she told him. "You don't stay in one place long enough to give her a home."

Babe retaliated, "You can't have her. She's mine and I'll keep her."

My father, fearful of a potentially ugly legal battle, decided to take matters into his own hands. One cold night in the middle of January, a week after Helen's death, two nuns woke me up and told me to get dressed and pack all my belongings. I had no idea what was going on, but I did what I was told.

The next thing I knew, I was boarding a train bound for New York with two nuns who kept saying, "Trust in God: Everything will be all right." When I heard that, I knew I was in trouble.

When we arrived in New York the next morning, I was placed in the New York Foundling Hospital on East 68th Street, where I was abandoned once again. I spent the day wandering around the hospital, broken-hearted, staring at all the unfamiliar faces—mostly children who looked even more despondent and confused than I did. No one paid much attention to me, but then I was used to that. It was strange how I could feel so left out among so many people.

After a sleepless, terrifying night in a sterile, faceless room with tall ceilings and dark shadows, I was taken to see Sister

Xavier, the mother superior at the Foundling Hospital. She told me that I was going to live with a nice lady named Miss Dooley, one of the workers at the hospital, until my father came for me.

Miss Dooley lived in a three-story brownstone in Brooklyn. One of her first acts as my temporary guardian was to inform me that my name would no longer be Dorothy Helen Ruth but Marie Harrington. I was defiant and insisted that my name was Dorothy Ruth, but it was no use. She wrote "Marie Harrington" in all my books and on all my clothes. I went to school with Marie Harrington embroidered across my gym suit. Hester Prynne had only one scarlet letter—I had fifteen. But believe it or not, I felt sorry for Miss Dooley, because I was a far cry from a cooperative, well-mannered nine-year-old. I woke up every morning with a scowl on my face, and after three months with her I felt certain that surgery would be needed to remove it.

You can imagine my bewilderment, not knowing where Helen or my father was, or why I was living with this strange woman under a different name. I was never told the reason for all the secrecy, but I have to believe it was an extra precaution which my father took to ensure retaining custody of me in case the courts ruled against him.

Meanwhile, there was a great deal of interest in locating Helen's will. She died a wealthly woman, and her relatives were fearful that Dr. Kinder or Babe would be entitled to a generous portion of her estate, depending on when the will had been executed. Coincidentally, one day before Helen died, Babe had mailed her a $25,000 check which represented the final payment of their $100,000 separation agreement. Since the envelope was postmarked January 10, 1929, the day before Helen died, it was legally her money and became part of her estate.

The reading of the will took place on January 29, 1929, and created quite a stir. Helen had left her mother, her seven brothers and sisters, and my father five dollars a piece. It came as no surprise that my father was slighted, but her own family? No one knew the reasoning behind this.

To the astonishment of everyone, Helen bequeathed her entire estate, $50,000, "to my beloved ward, Dorothy Helen Ruth." By referring to me as her ward, she was admitting publicly—for the first time—that I was not her real daughter.

Well, if Helen wasn't my mother, then who was?

5

A Rude Awakening

One day Miss Dooley took me back to the Foundling Hospital—my father was at last coming to see me! I was sitting by myself in a drab, gray waiting room when suddenly the door flew open and Dad, bigger than life, bounded into the room. The scowl I had been wearing for five months turned into the biggest, brightest smile my face could manage, and I jumped from my chair, ran across the room and leaped into his outstretched arms. I didn't think anything in the world could spoil our reunion—but I was wrong.

I sensed that something wasn't quite right, and when I lifted my head slightly and glanced over his shoulder, I saw a dark-haired woman standing behind him. As she approached, my father said, "Claire is going to be your new mother."

"Where is my real mother?" I howled over and over again. When neither of them answered, I started crying and ran for the open door. My father was one step ahead of me and grabbed me by the arm, lifting me back into his arms. He tried to calm me down, but it was no use—I was like a wild animal. All the rage I had suppressed for years came to a head at that moment. "She is not my mother, and she'll never be my mother!"

Claire then handed me a doll, which she had brought me as a gift. I took the doll and tore off the wig, poked its eyes out, ripped the arms off, and threw it on the floor. Claire, momentarily stunned by my outburst, chose to do nothing about it. Neither did my father, who told me that as soon as he and Claire were married, I would be coming to live with them on Riverside Drive, in Manhattan. As I sat there fuming, I thought to myself, well, I guess the world hasn't seen the last of my scowl.

During my five-month stay with her, Miss Dooley told me that my mother had gone to heaven, and that I had inherited $50,000, which was put in a trust fund for me. Helen's death made little impression on me at the time. Part of the reason, I think, was that my disposition had changed from the warmth and friendliness of my early years to cold distance. Being confined like a prisoner for so many years in different institutions, without any love or guidance, made me hostile and resentful. I had few friends, and I was tired of strangers trying to "help" me. During my formative years, I formed a shell, which became more and more impenetrable as time went by.

On April 17, 1929, exactly three months and six days after Helen's death, Babe and Claire were married at St. Gregory's Roman Catholic Church on West 90th Street. The wedding was supposed to be a secret and therefore was held at 5:45 A.M. But since nothing my father ever did remained a secret for long, he ended up signing baseballs for the altar boys and posing for pictures before greeting a crowd of approximately two thousand well-wishers outside the church after the service. When a reporter asked where the couple was going on their honeymoon, Claire responded, "We're not going on a honeymoon. We're going to work to win another pennant."

April 17 was also opening day of the 1929 season at Yankee Stadium, and the groom, not wanting to disappoint a packed house, was out in his familiar right-field position. During the game, he walloped a home run into the right-field bleachers and then blew a kiss to Claire, who was seated behind the Yankee dugout. The young bride, however, did not approve of the gesture and told him so after the game. "You'd better stop blowing kisses," she scolded, "or you're gonna be hearing about it from everybody in the league."

Dad's second wife could not possibly have been more different than his first. Claire was a sultry beauty with dark brown hair, lush red lips, piercing brown eyes, skin like satin and a superb figure. Facially she resembled sex-symbol Jean Harlow, minus the platinum-blonde hair. She had expensive taste in clothes and always wore high heels; at night she used rubber stockings to keep her legs firm and shapely.

Claire was only five feet two, but she looked taller; she always seemed to be up on a pedestal, looking down at the rest of the world. When she posed for photographers, she would give come-hither looks, yet if you met her on the street you would be struck by her aloofness. She was a woman who knew what she wanted and exactly how to go about getting it. And everywhere she went, she let it be known that she was *Mrs. Babe Ruth.*

Over the years, Claire's actions made it clear that she was protecting her "investment." I believe she loved my father and did have his best interests at heart when they were first married, but gradually her desire for money, power and prestige led that love astray. She was soon placing restrictions on Babe's extravagant lifestyle and treating him more like a naughty schoolboy than a baseball hero. "A bride can do an awful lot with her husband of a few months that a wife of ten years can't do," she would say in her high-pitched voice, which always made someone do a double-take when hearing it for the first time. In many instances her iron glove was not necessary, but this was the beginning of Claire's plan to assume control of Dad's life.

At the time Babe's affairs were being competently managed by Christy Walsh. Walsh was a good friend, an honest man and a wizard when it came to managing money. But his talents did not stop there. Christy also served as Dad's ghostwriter, promoter, legal advisor and accountant. Without him, Dad would have spent every nickel he earned, as fast as he earned it. It was Christy who set up the trust funds that assured my father's financial security when he retired. He also compiled a scrapbook for me entitled "Little Miss Babe," which I never knew existed until after Claire died. I discovered it in the garbage while I was cleaning out her apartment. My past was never of any concern to Claire.

Claire considered Christy a threat; therefore, she "politely" discharged him. Dad was upset, but there was nothing he could do. Captain Claire was at the helm.

Adjusting to Claire's new regime was going to be Babe's greatest challenge. She had a new word for Dad's vocabulary: moderation. Years later, she explained the difficult task with which she felt presented in a book, *The Babe and I*: "Now that I was Mrs. Ruth, I felt Mrs. Ruth had a job to do. It's the job every wife does in one form or another, I imagine, no matter how many of them insist upon denying it. I had a few reforms to institute."

Dad continued to excel on the field from 1929 through 1933, averaging more than 40 home runs and 140 RBIs, with a .340 batting average. And as long as Babe was producing on the field, Claire was content. It may be a coincidence, I can't be sure, but Babe and Claire's marriage definitely suffered once Dad was out of baseball.

Up until they married, my father had approached life the same way he approached hitting a baseball: "I swing with everything I've got." He figured that when he died, life wasn't going to owe him two seconds. I can remember as a little girl that he would drink a highball, smoke a cigar and chew tobacco—all at the same time. I was the first one out of the room when he did that. Bootleggers would bring cases of liquor wrapped in burlap bags and old newspapers to the apartment for him; those cases had sat in the Hudson River for days, and boy, was there a stench!

My new mother had no use for my father's drinking or his old drinking buddies. She felt they were hindering his performance on the field and merely waiting for the right opportunity to take advantage of him. I believe she used the term "moochers." Claire was a lot tougher than either of his Yankee managers, Miller Huggins and Joe McCarthy: their curfew was around midnight, Claire's was 10:00 P.M. She wrote in her book, "I recall one swank penthouse party we attended where the host set back his clocks. He neglected to take the precaution, however, of setting back my wristwatch."

In regard to Babe's eating habits, there was little chance of any repeat performance of "The Stomach Ache Heard 'Round the World," the legendary tale of one of Babe's hot dog and soda pop binges which landed him in a hospital bed for more than a week. One time my father came down with another serious stomach ache after eating eight or nine hot dogs, a few bags of peanuts and an apple, and washing it all down with five sodas. As he finished chugging down a pint of bicarbonate of soda, he sheepishly explained, "I'm sure it was that apple which upset my stomach."

As far as Claire was concerned, ballpark food—hot dogs, peanuts—was now off limits. But when Babe was in uniform, Claire was no longer able to supervise his diet. While she was in the stands cheering, he was at the concession stand, indulging in his favorite treats with the delight of a little boy.

Claire also curbed his spending, which was outlandish, to say the least. He would often leave a fifty-dollar tip for a fifty-cent sandwich, and one time, albeit unintentionally, he tipped a cabdriver a thousand dollars. Babe had four thousand-dollar bills in his wallet from a good showing at the track and paid the driver quickly, thinking he was only giving him a ten-dollar bill. He realized his mistake when he got home but was unfazed by the incident. One of his favorite sayings was "I've spent over a half million dollars, and I haven't the faintest idea what I've spent it on." Most of the money was undoubtedly spent before Claire started writing the checks and tightening the reins on the Ruth budget.

My father's other vices were quickly becoming distant memories. In the winter of 1920 he lost $40,000 in Cuba at the racetrack. A dollar to him was like a penny, but Claire delivered the ultimatum, "You'll have to give up the racing form or me." She objected to his camel-hair cap as well, but Babe won that battle and continued to wear it religiously for years.

She even traveled with the club on road trips, which was unheard of at the time, and screened all of his phone calls, many of which were from amorous women. One funny story, told to me by one of Babe's teammates, concerned the potential hazards of flirting. The Yankees were all sitting in a train car, waiting to leave the station, when all of a sudden Dad comes sprinting through the car with Claire in hot pursuit. She was holding a knife and yelling, "If I ever get a hold of you, I'll cut it off!" The Yankees were all laughing hysterically, so I imagine she was just having some "fun."

My father's days of reckless abandon were over. He was going to have to get used to life as a domesticated husband —except that Claire acted more like his mother than his wife. And I was the one who needed a mother!

About two months after their marriage, I joined Babe and Claire on Riverside Drive. Once again, my name was Dorothy Helen Ruth, and I began yet another chapter in my life without anyone bothering to tell me what had happened to Helen. I found that out myself—by accident. The following year, while putting together a scrapbook of my father's newspaper clippings with Claire's mother, Carrie, I discovered all the stories about Helen dying in a mysterious fire. Neither Claire nor Babe ever had the decency to tell me what had happened.

Babe and Claire eventually rented a fourteen-room apartment on the seventh floor at 345 West 88th Street. It was a spacious, inhospitable apartment, probably over three thousand square feet, for which Claire had chosen apple-green walls, chartreuse ceilings and furniture from all different periods—making it obvious that she knew very little about interior decorating. Even the Oriental rugs, lithographs and draperies failed to give the rooms character or sentiment. The only time the apartment warmed up was when my father walked in the door; his presence alone could fill the cold hollows.

My father had the only plush chair in the apartment; it sat in his bedroom next to the window, at arm's length from his brass spittoon and Philco radio. He loved to sit in the chair, gaze down at the Hudson River and listen to his favorite radio programs, such as "Gangbusters," "The Shadow" and, last but not least, "The Lone Ranger." The walls of his room were bare save for a plaque of St. Theresa, which was draped with two sets of rosary beads, given to him by the brothers of St. Mary's Industrial School for Boys, where he spent the better part of his youth.

Claire's two brothers, Eugene and Hubert, and her mother, Miss Carrie Merritt, also shared the apartment with us. I was thankful that they did, because it would be Carrie, Hubert and Eugene, not Claire and Julia, who would treat me with kindness and understanding over the next ten years. Of course, this had to be done discreetly, lest Claire find out.

Both Hubert and Eugene were in their mid-forties, had fought in World War I, and were no taller than five foot ten. Hubert was the more outgoing of the two. He had blond hair, blue eyes, fair skin and a medium build. Eugene worked nights, so during the day I saw more of Hubert. He would often take my girlfriend Carolyn and me to Jones Beach, on Long Island, when he had some spare time. One time we got such severe sunburns that we could only lie on my bed, face down, while Hubert placed tea bags on our backs to ease the pain. Dad poked his head in the door every twenty minutes or so to check on our condition.

Eugene, the elder of the two brothers, had been poisoned by the Germans during World War I, while fighting in the Argonne woods. The lethal gases from the bombing raids gradually destroyed his lungs. He rarely complained, but I could tell that he was in constant pain. I watched as his spirit dwindled and the end approached. Then, one quiet Sunday morning in 1933, while I did my homework in my room, the doorman rang the bell and told Carrie that Eugene was on the pavement—he had jumped fifteen stories.

Carrie was devastated. Only twelve at the time, I was more stunned than anything else. I wanted to comfort Carrie, say something to her to make her feel better, but she was already so upset that I was afraid of saying the wrong thing. Instead, I hugged her tightly and cried.

Carrie called Babe and Claire in Florida, where Dad was preparing for spring training; shocked and saddened, he took the next train to New York to make the funeral arrangements. Claire remained in Florida, apparently unaffected by the tragedy. Dad was lost; other people had always taken care of the details for him. In this case, Charlie and Juanita Ellias, close friends of Babe and Claire, helped him with the arrangements.

Dad was concerned that Carrie and I would not be able to manage with only Hubert to take care of us, so he told us to pack our bags and come to live with him and Claire in Florida. After the funeral, we took the train down, and he enrolled me in Aikens Open Air School in St. Petersburg. The warm weather, classes under the palm trees, and long walks on the beach with Dad were a welcome change of pace from the claustrophobia of our city apartment. I had more friends there than I had ever had in New York, and I wished that we could remain in Florida forever. No such luck. The opening of the season was in April, and that signaled my return to New York.

As the months went by, my position in my new mother's heart became clear: I was excess baggage. Raising me was a burdensome job, like a stack of unexpected paperwork dropped in her lap. Claire's favoritism toward her own daughter, Julia, created a no-win situation, one with which I regretfully would have to cope for the next ten years.

Julia and I were sisters, but not in the true sense of the word; we slept under the same roof and ate at the same table, but that's all we had in common. Claire had every intention of raising Julia in her own image. If you look at photographs of them from the early 1930s, you will see that they appear almost identical. Claire felt that there was no reason why her daughter should not have the best of everything. Even fifty-five years later, at an Old Timers Day luncheon at Yankee Stadium, one of the players' wives who remembered me as a little girl reminisced, "Nothing was too good for Julia. You were lucky if you received the time of day." I went to public schools, while Julia went to exclusive private schools. She traveled constantly all over the country, while I was rarely allowed out of my room. Julia could shop at fancy stores like Bergdorf-Goodman, while I was given hand-me downs—and not from Bergdorf-Goodman, either. She had her friends and I had mine.

Every time Claire accompanied Babe to spring training, she would take Julia out of school in New York and enroll her in Florida. My enrollment always stayed in New York. On the home front, her room was next to Claire's in our apartment; mine overlooked a courtyard and had previously been the maid's room.

Julia was thirteen years old when I met her, and I was in such a foul mood for so long that I never really gave her a chance. I can't blame her for our lack of communication, and Dad was busy with all his commitments and didn't know what was going on. I blame Claire. Julia wanted to be my friend, but Claire manipulated her emotions in such a way that Julia began looking at me as a second-class citizen. Julia had a mind of her own, but Claire did not let her use it. Because I was the underdog, I did everything I could to hold on to my father by taunting Julia with words like "He's my daddy, not yours." I know that was cruel, but as an insecure, helpless ten-year-old, words were my only weapon.

It was very important to Claire that the public have a wholesome image of the Ruth family, so what went on behind closed doors stayed behind closed doors. One of the big tests of this policy was the party that Dad threw for the newspapermen each year. I always enjoyed the occasion a great deal because the writers paid so much attention to me, and this would really make Claire squirm; in fact, she would usually dispatch me to my room after a while to remedy the situation. By the end of the night, the wastepaper baskets would be filled with used flashbulbs, and Dad loved to drop them onto the sidewalk, fifteen stories down, and watch them explode.

Before I was sent to my room I would always have a great time. The writers loved to hear the point of view of a little girl, and I felt that they were the only ones who ever wanted to hear what I had to say. I used to hold the attention of some of the greatest sportswriters of the century, such as Damon Runyon, Freddy Lieb and Grantland Rice. I particularly remember Rice, a soft-spoken gentleman who was probably the most widely read sportswriter of the day; he had a warm smile and classy good looks. Dan Parker, Ken Smith, Charlie Segar, Ed Sullivan, the future variety-show legend, and Marshall Hunt also came around, as did cartoonist Burris Jenkins. Hunt was my father's shadow. One year he followed my father to Hot Springs, Arkansas, and, in order to keep Babe in sight, actually took a steam bath in the tub next to him.

It was priceless to see Claire in action on the day the press arrived. "Dorothy sweetie, would you please get the dip for the gentleman?" she would say with a pleasant, phony smile. Or, "Please dear, would you get mother a glass of water?" It was all I could do to keep from throwing up. Once the newspapermen left, everything was back to normal. "Dorothy! Get out of the kitchen!" she would scream. "Didn't I tell you to go to your room?" What a transformation: Dr. Jekyll and Mrs. Ruth.

In order to unify the "family," Babe adopted Julia, who was then about fourteen, and Claire adopted me. The official papers were signed January 14, 1930. Claire did not want me to have any advantage that Julia did not, since now we were at least *legal* sisters, so she insisted that my father deposit $50,000 of his own money in a trust fund for Julia. Babe was shocked and adamantly refused. This created even more animosity between Claire and me, especially since Claire would use the money in my trust fund to pay for my clothes; she would simply get a lawyer to petition the courts to gain access to my estate. She was envious that I had so much money of my own; to Claire, money was synonomous with superiority. (Years later, this preferential treatment continued. In 1938, when Julia was getting married, Claire wanted Dad to give her $50,000 and a Buick coupé. Dad refused, and Julia only received the car.)

But the only time our family ever really acted like one was during a crisis, and most of the time this involved my father's health. In 1931 he was hurt sliding into home plate and hospitalized for five days with a paralyzed nerve in his leg. The three of us put aside our animosities for the visit to the hospital and tried to present a unified front in our desire to comfort him.

There were many instances like that one. Dad had a history of catching terrible colds and flus—even pneumonia. He once had a fever of 105 degrees and lost about forty pounds. He never dressed warmly enough, got enough sleep, ate the right foods, or took care of his body—unimaginable for today's athlete. Consequently, he ran up some pretty hefty hospital bills in his lifetime.

Outside of these times of united worry, I lived my life, Claire and Julia lived theirs, and Babe lived his.

DAILY NEWS

NEW YORK'S PICTURE NEWSPAPER

FINAL EDITION

Average net paid circulation of THE NEWS, Dec., 1928:
Sunday, 1,571,092
Daily, 1,253,391

Copyright 1929 by News Syndicate Co. Inc. Reg U S Pat Off

Entered as 2nd class matter Post Office New York, N.Y.

Vol. 10. No. 173 36 Pages   New York, Monday, January 14, 1929   2 Cents IN CITY LIMITS   3 CENTS Elsewhere

MRS. BABE RUTH DIES IN LOVE NEST FIRE

Story on Page 3

Firemen search ruins of house at Watertown, Mass., where Mrs. George Herman Ruth, wife of Babe, died of suffocation in fire. She was the former Miss Helen Woodford, whom Babe met in Boston. —(By A. & A. T. & T. transmission)

In happier days. Babe's wife and daughter come to the Pennsylvania station to see Sultan of Swat off on trip to Hot Springs, Va., to round into shape. —(NEWS photo)

UP, PLEASE!—Highest blaze in city's history puzzled firemen yesterday when flames broke out on 57th floor of Woolworth building. Ladders useless, firemen had to wait for lifts to take them to scene of fire. —*Story on page 2.*   (NEWS photo)

BABE'S WIFE DIES!—Body of woman found in fire at Watertown, Mass., was identified as that of Mrs. Babe Ruth, wife of slugger. They had been separated for some time.—*Story on page 2.*

57th Story of Woolworth Building Afire. PAGE TWO

6

Claire Declares War

By the early 1930s my father's popularity had reached an all-time high, and the demands on his time were endless. I had to realize that, with all his commitments, I was not going to be his number-one priority. We did not have the intimate relationship that many fathers and daughters shared.

Because he did not spend as much time with me as most fathers would have, the times we did share were all the more special: decorating the Christmas tree, playing cards, going on picnics on his days off, or listening to "The Lone Ranger" on the radio. He loved to come home and throw his huge raccoon coat at me to see if I could catch it—which was almost impossible, since the coat weighed more than I did. I would always end up on the floor underneath the coat, while my father laughed and laughed.

If I was lucky he would take me on roadtrips, usually to Boston, Philadelphia or Washington, D.C. His teammates Ben Chapman, Lefty Gomez and Frank Crosetti did their best to entertain me on the train rides by singing songs. During these trips I was incredibly happy; my father would call me "Butch" and "Duck," but when he was angry it was always "Dorothy."

Sometimes the Yankees would send Dad five or six dozen balls at a time for him to autograph. My job was to make sure that the ink from the fountain pen did not smear. Then, when the balls dried, I would rewrap them and put them back in the box.

During my trips to Yankee Stadium and the parties in our apartment, I became friendly with some of the newspapermen, especially Rudd Rennie of the *New York Herald Tribune.* Dad enjoyed talking to the media and realized it was an important part of his job, but sometimes his actions were top secret. Chances were, you could always get a good story if you could find Babe, but finding him was sometimes a good story in itself. His car was rarely parked in front of the apartment; instead it was spotted at some of the strangest locations in the city, at all hours of the evening. I was told that one time he met a lady friend at a red light, left his car in the middle of the street and drove away with her!

To eliminate constant surveillance on his apartment, a couple of newspapermen gave me a telephone number to call whenever I overheard my father's plans. For my information, I was rewarded with much thanks and—more important to me at the time—attention. As soon as he left, I would call that number and tip them off. When my father came home he would always say, "Those writers are unbelievable. How the hell do they know where I'm going before I ever get there?" He never did find out how they knew. However, to some degree the writers, because they idolized him, protected Dad's reputation by keeping the worst of his escapades out of print.

Every morning Babe left the apartment at 7:30 A.M. and did not return until 7:30 P.M. for dinner. As soon as he walked in the door, I would run up and kiss him. As a child, I kissed my father often, a practice I never grew tired of in later years. I felt very safe in his arms, but Claire gradually began to discourage my behavior, saying, "Don't hang all over your father. Can't you see how tired he is?" Claire was so insecure that she saw me as competition, and, in her mind, only she was allowed to get close to my father. I was constantly reprimanded and punished for trying to do the same thing. She was intent on alienating Babe from everyone who cared for him—and whom he cared about. After a while, her efforts were successful.

My father rarely took me to Yankee Stadium, but when he did, I would ride with him and Claire in the back seat of his Cadillac. Once at the game Claire tried to keep me away from the sportswriters, and she would not let me eat peanuts, ice cream or candy. Once the game started I had to be quiet because she would not allow yelling at the opposing batters. What fun was going to a baseball game if I couldn't do any of those things? It got to the point where so many restrictions were placed on me that I no longer enjoyed going; when it was time to leave for Yankee Stadium, I would sneak out of the apartment and hide in Riverside Park until my father and Claire were gone.

I had my own interests, and baseball wasn't one of them. I played touch football, stick hockey and stoopball—tomboy activities that most definitely did not meet with Claire's approval. In fact, I was never a doll-and-carriage type of girl. I was the only girl in the neighborhood whom the boys allowed in their company. My adventurous spirit intrigued them. Just like Dad, if someone dared me to do something, I was eager to accept the challenge; I was indestructible, and life was only a game. In order to prove myself to the boys, I walked along ledges nine stories above the ground, played on train tracks and recklessly hurled myself down steep hills on homemade sleds. One time I narrowly escaped serious injury when my sled crashed head-on into a tree. Luckily, I bailed out at the last minute. I wish I could say the same for my friend Carolyn, who suffered a sprained ankle and a bloody nose.

Claire constantly watched for me to step out of line in the slightest way. Any transgression could be used to demean me in my father's eyes. "Did you see what Dorothy did?" Claire would spitefully tell Babe. "Julia would never do something like that."

It's a good thing Claire never found out about one of my more mischievous adventures. Carolyn and I found the perfect half of an eggshell and decided to place it upside down over the drain of an outdoor goldfish fountain. The drain clogged and the water and fish overflowed the fountain's edges. We hid in a corner, watching the maintenance men frantically try to retrieve flapping goldfish from all over the courtyard. When Caroline's mother heard of our escapade, she said, "If you and Dorothy go to jail, who's going to bail you out?" Carolyn answered, "Don't worry, Babe would bail us both out. I'm Dorothy's best friend, so he'd never leave me in there."

I wanted a bicycle more than anything else when I was a kid, but Claire refused to buy me one. One day I borrowed a friend's and left it on Riverside Drive, where it got stolen. I searched every bicycle shop on Broadway and Amsterdam Avenue from 59th to 110th Street, without any luck. When Claire found out that my father would have to pay my friend's parents for the missing bike, she was furious and told me to never borrow anything again. That unfortunate incident cost me one week in my room.

I lived in one of the largest apartments in New York City, yet it felt like the smallest. My room was six feet by nine feet, and the only window faced a courtyard, where I could see the cooks from other households preparing meals while I did my homework on the bed. It was hard to gauge the time, since the window afforded only about an hour of sunlight a day. One picture decorated the walls, a baby print with the inscription "Mighty Like a Rose"; I found the print years later and have it hanging in my house today. There was no carpeting nor drapes in the room, only leftover, mismatched furniture. During my childhood, I spent so much time in that room that I used to know the exact number of flowers in the wallpaper, but mercifully I've forgotten since then.

I went to St. Gregory's Catholic School on 90th Street, between Amsterdam and Columbus, along with many of the poor children in the area who lived in railroad flats.

Many of their parents had been hard hit by the Depression and could not afford their heating bills during the winter. In order to help them, I went around the neighborhood one day with my friend Anna May on a coal-recycling drive, looking for unused pieces of coal on the sidewalk. My punishment for coming home with black hands, looking like a chimney sweep, was a "reasonable" one-month sentence in my room for what Claire termed "conduct unbecoming a lady." I never counted the days I spent in my cell, but my room definitely became my home away from home.

I never told my father about the way I was treated by Claire because I didn't think he would believe me, and he wasn't home enough to see it first-hand. He was busy traveling, making movies, visiting hospitals, speaking at benefits, or doing any of a number of activities which kept him away from home. And when he was home, Claire monopolized most of his time. I didn't ask him for money because I knew Claire controlled the family checkbook, and so there was little chance of getting a single cent.

Babe was a good father, given the circumstances. He never deliberately neglected me, and I know he loved me very much. He was just uncomfortable showing it, for fear of repercussions from Claire. So not only was I deprived of many of the tangible objects that were normal, expected parts of most little girls' lives—nice new clothes, a bicycle— but I also received little of the love and affection that any child needs while growing up. I know it may sound hard to believe, because it took me a long time to figure it out myself, but Claire had a hold on my father that would never be broken.

I found out later that, before Babe and Claire were married, they had lived together for seven years—while he was still married to Helen. It was reported in the press that Dad and Claire were close friends, but no one knew exactly how close the relationship went. Then it was morally inexcusable for a man and woman to live together without being married, so any rumors of their intimate relationship were quickly squelched by my father.

Claire grew tired of the mistress role after a while and threatened to expose the sordid details of their lengthy affair to the newspapers if my father did not marry her. Babe, fearful of a besmirched reputation, allowed himself to be blackmailed in this fashion.

Claire realized early on that her trump card was my father's perception of himself, and the fact that he truly believed that the evidence against him which Claire had accumulated over the years would be damaging to his career and reputation. Many of you reading this might think, "Why would an athlete as celebrated as Babe Ruth be so worried about Claire's threats?" To answer this question, I must explain how my father viewed himself and what he had to lose.

Dad did not see himself as an extraordinary person. Going to the ballpark was a job, much the same as everyone else's. He felt he was just an ordinary person trying to earn a living.

His good friends weren't the affluent and influential; they were cabdrivers, paperboys, doormen and small businessmen. Before every game he would stop at the corner fruit market on 168th and Lexington Avenue and buy a head of cabbage. He kept it on the bench in a bucket of ice and each inning wore a fresh leaf under his cap to keep cool.

Babe would not have enjoyed being chauffeured around in a stretch limousine with tinted windows, had they existed at the time; instead, he loved to drive down Broadway in a convertible, waving to the people. One of his favorite stops was at Seventh Avenue and 123rd Street in Harlem. There, a scoreboard in the window of a store gave updated out-of-town scores. Huge crowds would gather while he double-parked and waited for the scores.

The difference between my father and most celebrities was that Babe was approachable. That's one of the reasons he became the hero of the common man—he had time for everyone. But Claire wanted nothing to do with that aspect of his life. She resented his rubbing elbows with the working person, feeling that she and Babe were above everyone else. But my father never felt that way. The only time I ever remember him shunning autograph seekers was at Lou Gehrig's wake.

Babe was not impressed by foreign dignitaries or presidents and treated them as if they were also on his level. When he met Queen Wilhelmina of the Netherlands, he tapped her on the shoulder and said, "Hi ya, Queenie." He was not being disrespectful, only friendly. Another time he asked President Calvin Coolidge, "Hot as hell, ain't it, Prez?" And when he visited King George V of England, his friends and the king's staff tried to make him wear a morning suit, according to protocol. He said, "No thank you. I'll wear my blue suit and white silk shirt with the collar open. What's good enough for my president is good enough for your king."

Through it all, my father's greatest concern was "the little kids with the dirty faces," a reference to the less fortunate children who idolized him. As a youth Babe was no different, and he believed that his success gave every one of those kids hope for the future.

Even though Dad was thought of as god-like, he was really very down to earth. I guess he best represented Everyman; so in his mind, he did feel he had a lot to lose should Claire ever follow through with her idle threats.

ST. MARY'S INDUSTRIAL SCHOOL-WILKENS AVE.-BALTIMORE, MD.
FRITZ MAIZEL   BEN ROMANS   COCKY NITCH
JACK MACHEN   BABE RUTH   BRU BOCK
            SID OWENS   DIZZY TATE

Dad's St. Mary's Industrial School baseball team. The other members are (clockwise from upper righthand corner): Cocky Nitch, Bru Bock, Dizzy Tate, Sid Owens, Jack Machen, Fritz Maizel and Ben Romans. (photo courtesy National Baseball Library, Cooperstown, NY)

*General Pershing and Babe Ruth during a World War I
bond drive. (photo courtesy National Baseball Library,
Cooperstown, NY)*

Two great Americans, Babe Ruth and Will Rogers.

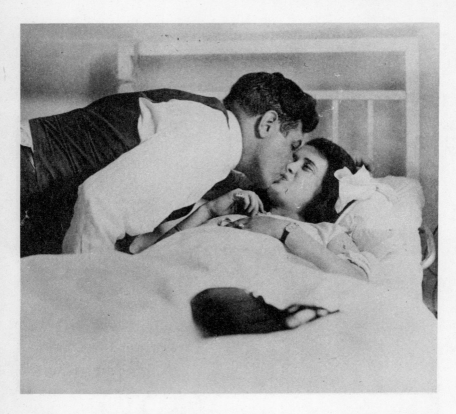

My father visiting Helen in the hospital, June 1922. She was in for minor surgery, he had just had his tonsils removed. Notice the dinner ring on her small finger.

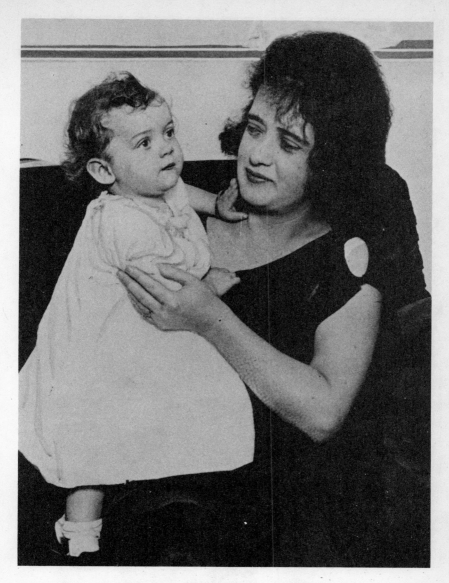

Here I am, making my debut with Helen in front of the newsmen.

Helen, Babe and I heading out for spring training.

"Let's play ball!" I'm a chip off the old block.

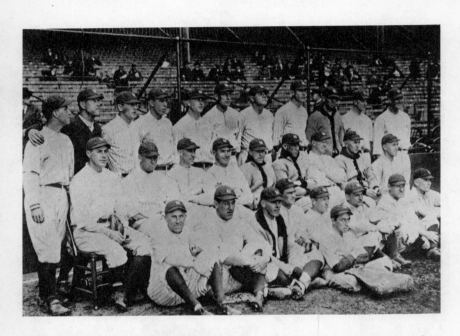

The 1924 New York Yankees: (top row, from left to right) Bengough, Bush, Haines, Hoffman, Hoyt, Pipp, Ruth, Hendrick, Roettger, Mahoney, Autry, (middle row) McNally, Schang, Dugan, Ward, Huggins, Jones, Witt, Shawkey, unknown, (bottom row) Johnson, Gehrig, Pipgras, Combs, O'Leary, Gazella, Urban, Olsen, Bennett (bat boy). (photo courtesy C. E. "Pat" Olsen)

The Yankees barnstorming in Sharon, Pennsylvania, in 1924. (photo courtesy National Baseball Library, Cooperstown, NY)

Home Plate Farm, in Sudbury, Massachusetts.

Some of my happiest days were spent with Dad on the Sudbury farm.

AGREEMENT

This agreement made the 4th day of August, 1925 by and between HELEN RUTH and GEO. H. RUTH. New York City.

WHEREAS, the parties hereto are married to each other for the last 7 months have lived separate and apart.

WHEREAS, the parties hereto have agreed to live separate and apart in the future, without molesting each other or interfering with each others actions how-so-ever and what-so-ever.

WHEREAS, the parties hereto agree that they cannot live together on account incomparibility of each party.

WHEREAS, the party hereto of the second party hereby agrees, to pay to the party of the first part the sum ONE HUNDRED DOLLARS PER WEEK and all maintenance in New York and at the farm in SUDBURY MASS. until such time as the first payment of the said agreement is made in October 1925.

WHEREAS, the party of the second part promises to pay to the party of the first part, One hundred thousand dollars, in the following payments:-

First payment - in October 1925 to be Twenty-thousand dollars.
Second payment - in October 1926 to be Thirty thousand dollars.
Third payment - in October 1927 to be twenty-five thousand dollars
Final payment - in October 1928 of twenty-five thousand dollars.

WHEREAS, the party of the second part, pro-

mises to pay to the party of the first part one half of the amount received from Mr. CHRISTY WALSH after Mr. CHRISTY WALSH has made necessary payment on the party of the second part's insurance policy which is in Mr. CHRISTY WALSH care. This payment is to be deducted from the original One hundred thousand dollars, included in agreement.

WHEREAS, the policy which the party of the second part has in the hands of Mr. CHRISTY WALSH is to be so secured that the party of the first part is to collect if the party of the second part defaults in his payments, as stated above.

WHEREAS, this policy be so fixed that the party of the second part cannot collect until the party of the first part releases to the party of the second, and the party of the first part cannot collect until the party of the first part proves that the party of the second part has defaulted in his payments as stated above.

WHEREAS, the farm at SUDBURY MASS. is to be turned over by the party of the second part to the party of the first part, and the party of the first part assumes the mortgage and is at liberty to dispose said farm as she so desires.

WHEREAS, the party of the first part is to sign over to the party of the second part the lots that are situated in PASEDENA FLA. and the party of the second part is at liberty to dispose of same as he so desires.

WHEREAS, the party of the second part is to turn over to the party of the first part Packard car now in possession of the party of the first part.

WHEREAS, DOROTHY RUTH, is to be given into custody of the party of the first part.

WHEREAS, all outstanding bills at the present time and up to the time of this agreement goes into effect is to be paid by the party of the second part. And it is further agreed that after first payment is made on the above agreement in the month of October 1925, party of the second part shall be released from all obligations except those specifically stated, in above agreement.

E. J. QUINN Witness

HELEN RUTH (L.S.)

GEORGE RUTH (L.S.)

State of New York }
County of Richmond } ss:

On the 4ᵗʰ day of August nineteen hundred and Twenty-Five be fore me came George H. Ruth and Helen Ruth to me known ro be the individuals described in, and who executed the foregoing instrument, and acknowledged that they executed the same.

The separation agreement of Babe and his first wife, Helen, dated August 4, 1925.

A star is born—Dad's publicity shot for The Babe Come Home. *He also appeared in* Pride of the Yankees, *the story of Lou Gehrig.*

My father would advertise anything—he was ahead of his time. Thank God that pantyhose had yet to be invented!

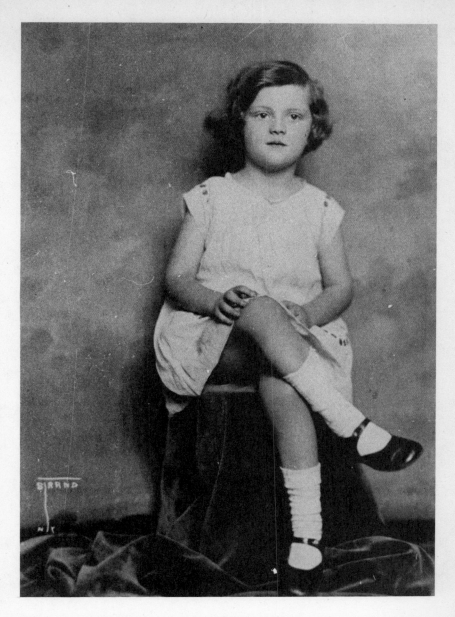

Dorothy Helen Ruth—or Marie Harrington—at seven years old. (photo by J. Anthony Lopez)

D.R.L. § 114

CERTIFICATE OF ADOPTION

STATE OF NEW YORK

COUNTY OF NEW YORK } ss.:

I, Robert M. Reaves, Chief Clerk of the Surrogate's Court of the said County, do hereby

certify that I have inspected the records of this Court in the matter of Adoptions and find that:

AN ORDER OF ADOPTION was signed on the   14   day of January   , 1930,

by HON.   JAMES A. FOLEY   Judge of the Surrogate's Court of the County

of New York granting the petition of   GEORGE HERMAN RUTH   and
CLAIRE HODGSON RUTH

his wife, then residing at   345 West 88th Street, N.Y.C.

for the adoption of a minor child now known and called by the name of DOROTHY RUTH
                                  (Court File No. 220/1930)
who was born at   N.Y.C.   on the   2nd   day of February   , 19 21

and directing that the child shall henceforth be regarded and treated in all respects as the child of said

petitioners.

IN TESTIMONY WHEREOF, I have hereunto set my hand and af-

fixed the seal of the Surrogate's Court of the County of New York

this   31   day of October   in the year of our Lord

one thousand nine hundred and eighty -six.

Robert M. Reaves
Chief Clerk of the Surrogate's Court of the County of New York

The certificate from my adoption by Claire.

The "happy" family posing for a newspaper photographer in the 1930s. (photo courtesy National Baseball Library, Cooperstown, NY)

I was about twelve or thirteen years old when this photograph was taken. This is what the newspapers saw. Funny, Claire didn't know how to play the piano. (photo courtesy National Baseball Library, Cooperstown, NY)

7

The Biggest Kid of Them All

To understand the unique relationship that my father shared with the children of the world, and the positive influence that he had on them, it is important to understand what life was like for Dad when he was growing up. Mamie Ruth, my father's sister, who at this writing is eighty-seven years old and lives in Hagerstown, Maryland, fondly remembered the early days in Baltimore with her brother, George, Jr.

"When I was in George's company, I used to have to look up at him until the back of my neck would ache, and he'd have to look down at me until the back of his neck ached.

"George wasn't a bad boy, he was a mischievous boy. The last thing you wanted to do was to dare George to do something. If you did, you might as well consider it done. Our father owned a saloon, but any of the rumors that George waited on the sailors is totally ridiculous. Neither of us were allowed anywhere near the bar.

"When Babe was old enough to hold a bat, we always knew where to find him—on the baseball diamond. His biggest problem was that he refused to go to school. Father insisted he get an education, but Babe deliberately disobeyed him. Daddy was forced to give him terrible whippings. My mother would say, 'George, don't whip him so hard. You may hurt him, and then you'll be sorry.' The whippings didn't do a bit of good. Babe was going to do what he wanted to do, no matter what the consequences.

"We went to the same school but we were not in the same class," Mamie continued. "My teacher would call me up to the front of her desk and say, 'Is George sick?' I'd reply, 'No, he's not sick. He went to school.' She'd respond, 'Well, he's not in school today. He must be playing hooky again.'

"Babe continued to do as he pleased. He wouldn't go to school, and that was that. The only way Daddy could rectify the situation was to send him someplace where they would force him to go to school. Then, when he was old enough, they'd send him out on his own."

Babe's father sent him to St. Mary's Industrial School, about four miles outside of downtown Baltimore. "The Home" was not an orphanage, as has frequently been rumored, but a place for runaways and incorrigibles, as well as orphans and children whose parents were divorced or separated.

"He was very content in St. Mary's once he realized it was the right place for him to be," recalled Mamie. "The brothers who ran St. Mary's were very good to him, especially Brother Matthias, the prefect of discipline, who was almost like a father to him. Matthias was an intimidating figure who commanded and received total respect from all the boys. He was close to six feet six inches tall and weighed around 240 pounds. He wore long, flowing black robes with a white sash around the mid-section. I was under five feet tall and scared to death whenever I'd stand next to him.

"George remained in St. Mary's until he was nineteen years old and signed his first professional baseball contract."

With the exception of an occasional visit home, Babe spent the better part of twelve years in St. Mary's, from the ages seven through nineteen. He viewed St. Mary's as his home and in later years defended the school vehemently when people would minimize its role in shaping his life. And other than his weight, his going to school in an "orphanage" was the easiest topic for players to goad Babe about during the course of an argument. In his autobiography he wrote, "I look back on St. Mary's as one of the most constructive periods of my life. I'm as proud of it as any Harvard man is proud of his school." He once spent more than a month of his spare time sponsoring the St. Mary's band on a tour through every city in the league in 1920, and he visited many of his old friends whenever he was in the Baltimore area.

Dad also confessed that as a boy he truly did not know the difference between right and wrong. "If my parents had something I wanted very badly, I took it," he said. My father may have taken things that didn't belong to him, but he seldom took them for himself. The money he managed to steal from his father's register was given to his poor friends in the neighborhood. He always seemed to root for the underdog, and had the firm conviction that giving was more important than receiving.

I think St. Mary's taught him to love children and to try and give them the guidance and affection that he never had growing up. Dad knew what it was like to grow up without parental guidance; his mother died of tuberculosis when he was only thirteen years old and his father was killed in an alley by muggers two years after Babe turned professional. In his adult years, much of his free time was spent visiting orphanages and children's wards. The terminally ill, the handicapped and the underprivileged were number one on his priority list. My father treasured these moments because he knew that some of the boys would not survive to see another of his visits.

He didn't always make a big entrance, either. Sometimes he would just stick his head in the room and look around, waiting for one of the boys to notice him. And then, wow! You'd never have known how sick some of those little fellows were. Every day was Christmas when Babe arrived, although on the actual day he would dress up as Santa Claus and surprise the kids with presents. He had a hearty laugh, as contagious as the common cold, bright eyes that lit up like a little boy's on Christmas morning, and a hefty paunch that needed little aid from a pillow.

His love for children was genuine. Lefty Gomez, a good friend and teammate of my father's, accompanied Babe on numerous good-will missions. "Babe visited dozens of hospitals because he loved children, not because he was looking for publicity. I knew plenty of hospitals that he went to that nobody knew about, which was the way he wanted it. I can still remember seeing those little guys lying in their beds until they'd spot Babe. All of a sudden, their faces would light up. Babe was probably the biggest kid of them all."

Some people said all his charity was a sham. Others spread rumors that he would show up intoxicated and only for money. That idle gossip couldn't have been any further from the truth. One of the premiere sportswriters of the day, Grantland Rice, remembered one story: "I went with Babe one day when he drove sixty miles before a World Series game in Chicago to visit a sick boy. And he told me when we returned that if I wrote one word about it, he'd knock my brains in."

Babe's bag of medicine didn't contain any miracle cures, only bats and promises to hit home runs. Some of his promises were well publicized, like the home run he hit for Johnny Sylvester in the 1926 World Series against the St. Louis Cardinals.

Johnny was eleven years old and lived in Essex Falls, New Jersey. He had been seriously injured in a fall, and doctors were not sure if he would pull through. In an effort to lift the boy's spirits, Johnny's father called Babe at Yankee Stadium and asked him if he would mind sending his son an autographed picture. Dad had an even better idea. Since the World Series wasn't scheduled to begin until the following day, he decided that he would visit the boy in person. Johnny, quite naturally, was a big Babe Ruth fan and kept a scrapbook filled with box scores and stories about Babe. Dad, true to his word, spent part of the day with Johnny and before leaving promised to hit a home run for him.

Babe did not live up to his promise immediately. He had only two hits in the first three games, but he did hit a record three home runs in the next game. Which one of those home runs were for Johnny is anybody's guess, but the fact remains that the boy recovered despite the doctors' predictions. As with a great deal of Babe Ruth lore, the exact details of the story differ in each account. In this story there are two facts that remain constant: Dad did visit Johnny Sylvester, and Johnny Sylvester did repay the favor some twenty years later as Dad lay dying in a New York hospital.

But most of Babe's promises never made it any further than the hospital room, although Mamie told me that she recently met a man for whom Babe had hit a home run at Yankee Stadium. Mamie remembered the home run, because she was there that day.

In 1929 sixty-two people, mostly children, were injured at Yankee Stadium while running for the exits during an electrical storm. Babe went the next day to Lincoln Hospital, armed with bats and balls. As he handed out presents to some of the injured children, one boy whispered to a friend, "Gee, I wish I'd been in that accident, maybe he'd give me a baseball."

Babe overheard the boy and inquired, "Why son, weren't you at Yankee Stadium that day?"

"No, Babe," answered the boy, "but I sure wish I had been."

"Well, here's a baseball anyway," said Dad, as he presented the boy with a ball, "just for being brave."

My father came away from many a hospital feeling as good as he had made the children feel, if not better. The children uplifted him, an experience that was missing from his personal life. But besides visiting hospitals, my father was also known to make house calls. One day, in Knoxville, Tennessee, a farmer approached Babe at an exhibition game and asked him to sign a ball for his sick boy at home.

It was dreary and overcast that day, with a threat of rain in the air. "Just hang around for an hour," Babe told the man. "I don't think we'll play today. Come back in an hour and we'll talk about going to see your boy."

It did rain that day, and the game was called. When my father returned from the clubhouse, the man was standing in the dugout holding the ball. "All right," laughed Babe. "Let's go and see the kid." Dad drove fifty miles out in the country and spent the entire afternoon with the boy.

My father's compassion for children was also felt around the world. A few years ago, I was given a touching picture of Babe reaching out to about a dozen blind children at a railroad station in Japan. What more need I say?

Why were so many children instinctively drawn to my father? How could he relate to them so naturally? One reason was because they spoke the same language, a language of innocence. Dad could truly be himself around kids and did not have to worry about the repercussions of saying or doing something wrong. During a normal day, anything he said could and would be used against him in the newspaper the next day.

For example, Dad did not involve himself in politics, but presidential candidates through the years welcomed the free publicity of a photograph taken with America's living legend. Babe declined to pose with President Herbert Hoover in 1928 because he favored Al Smith, a Democrat, for the presidency. However, earlier in the week a reporter had stated erroneously that Dad was backing Hoover, a rumor that my father staunchly denied. The following day the headlines screamed, "Ruth Refuses To Pose With Hoover." The Yankees forced Babe to apologize for what was an unintentional snub and arranged for the two to be photographed the next day.

My father in no way posed a threat to the children. He didn't represent an authoritative figure, like a school-teacher, principal or parent, telling them how to sit, how to act, or what to say. He wasn't intimidating. He didn't stare at them or try and enforce rules. Remember, the saying "Children were meant to be seen and not heard" was still very much believed by a society which had so recently left the Victorian era.

Another reason for Dad's popularity with children was that he was just a big kid himself: making faces, laughing, patting them on the head, cuddling them, or telling a story. Children really responded to his spontaneity. The sight of Babe, followed by dozens of boys while he signed autographs all the way to his car, was a common one. Some of his favorite kids were the "knot-hole gang" out in right field, a group of boys who regularly watched the game from a hole in the fence outside Yankee Stadium.

Dad tried to set a good example by telling boys to stay in school and obey their parents. The memories of his own rebellious youth were still sharp, and he believed that the time he devoted to children would not be in vain. If only one boy straightened out his life, it would be worth it.

On May 28, 1935, two days before he would play his final game in the major leagues, Dad suffered through one of the most humiliating experiences of his career. He was playing left field for the Boston Braves that day in a game against the Cincinnati Reds. In the fifth inning, the Reds batted around, scoring five runs on six hits, with almost every player in the lineup deliberately hitting the ball to my father. It was obvious how vulnerable he had become in the outfield at the late stage of his career.

Hall of Fame broadcaster Red Barber was then in his rookie year as a broadcaster with the Cincinnati Reds. In an article for *American Magazine* in 1947, Red remembered the circumstances that day as Dad dejectedly left the field, voluntarily removing himself from the game.

"Babe returned the ball and walked in slowly," Red reminisced. "Not to the dugout but to a passage in the stands. It led to the clubhouse showers. The stands were full of yelling, booing, hissing fans. The Babe had a look of darkest anger on his face. Mixed with it as he plodded along was an expression of bitter disappointment. But the old lion of the ball clubs showed he could still hit anything life had to pitch.

"In the midst of all that howling and jeering, a little boy toddled down the passage and clutched at the great player's knees. Ruth didn't hesitate a second. He picked up the kid and hugged him to his chest. Then he set the boy down with a pat on the head and went to the clubhouse.

"That went down in my book as a home run, Babe's 715th. The fans saw it that way too. They hushed immediately."

8

Chief Big Bat and Chief Little Bat

Ruth and Gehrig. Pinstripe power at its legendary best. They were the pride and joy of the New York Yankees for ten glorious years, from 1925 to 1934. Babe was boisterous, outspoken and extroverted. Lou was soft-spoken and introverted. And their home-run swings were as different as their personalities. Babe hit towering fly balls which seemed as though they would never come down. Lou smashed vicious line drives which threatened to rip the gloves off defenders. In Oklahoma an Indian tribe named Babe Ruth and Lou Gehrig Chief Big Bat and Chief Little Bat, respectively.

The two began their reign of terror over American League pitchers in the Roaring Twenties, when they roared louder than any other one-two punch in the history of baseball. Together they formed baseball's greatest partnership. On the field they were the most feared hitters of the day. Off the field they were inseparable companions.

My father and Lou were teammates in the true sense of the word. They competed for World Series Championships, not the spotlight. There was always room for another World

Series ring, not petty jealousies. Lou played in the shadow of the greatest showman the game has ever known yet never resented a minute of Babe's glory, although when asked what it was like, Gehrig responded, "It's a pretty big shadow." He also said that Babe was one of his best friends on the Yankee squad.

The crowds and media longed for a heated rivalry between the home-run twins, but the boys realized that any conflict amongst themselves would be counterproductive to the team. Their camaraderie was evident during their heyday, when they made a famous pact regarding four-baggers: the motto was "That's one for us." When my father was injured, he still yelled encouragement from the dugout. Babe had the utmost respect and admiration for Lou's ability, and one day paid him his highest praise: "If anyone is going to break my home-run record, it will be the Dutchman." Most of all, I think, they were two big kids who loved playing baseball more than anything else in the world.

In 1920 Babe was busy rewriting the record books daily with the Yankees at the Polo Grounds, while Lou was playing baseball at the High School of Commerce in Manhattan. In June of that year, at Wrigley Field in Chicago, Lane Technical High School of Chicago played Lou's High School of Commerce to decide the inter-city baseball championship. In the waning moments of that game, a broad-shouldered seventeen-year-old stepped to the plate and crushed the first pitch over the right-field fence for a grand slam to win the game. It was quite an accomplishment for a high school kid to hit a ball out of a major league park. That evening, for the first time, Lou Gehrig received national recognition. One writer hailed him as the schoolboy Ruth, and, also for the first time, Lou's name was linked to my father's.

In 1922 Lou enrolled in Columbia University in New York on a football scholarship; in fact, he played every game of the Fall 1922 schedule. But it was his titanic home runs that soon made him a legend. Many of these went over the trees and landed on Morningside Heights, an avenue across the street from Columbia's home field. One day he hit a ball that some say was still going when it shattered a window in the School of Journalism, some 425 feet from home plate. It wasn't long before major league scouts got wind of his heroics, particularly in New York. With a potential star in their own backyard, the Yankees assigned one of their scouts, Paul Krichell, to monitor Gehrig's progress.

In the spring of 1923, at New Brunswick, Gehrig hit another monstrous home run, prompting Krichell to eagerly phone Edward Grant Barrow, then the business manager of the Yankees, at his office in Yankee Stadium. "Ed! I think I found another Babe Ruth," he cried. Barrow laughed heartily and hung up. The next day, Lou swatted another tape-measure shot; this time the victim was one of the best pitchers in the East. The ball landed on the steps of the library across 116th Street. With that, Krichell approached Lou after the game and asked him if he wanted to play for the Yankees. Lou was a good student and dedicated to his studies, but when baseball called, he jumped at the opportunity, signing with the Yankees for $1,500 against the wishes of both his parents. As it turned out, Lou used this $1,500 bonus to pay for an operation which saved his father's life.

Lou and Babe first met in 1923, the same year Yankee Stadium opened. Lou was a sensitive, shy twenty-year-old who stood in awe of my father, who meanwhile was in the midst of one of his greatest seasons, the only year in which he would win the MVP award. Even though Babe was a celebrity, he still had plenty of time for the media, the fans and the younger players who demanded his attention. He took an immediate interest in Lou. Ford Frick, a baseball commissioner and one of my dad's biographers, said, "Ruth worried much more about Gehrig than he did about himself. Lou was embarrassed by the fatherly advice Ruth would often shower upon him publicly and privately."

In Lou's first at-bat as a Yankee, he struck out swinging on three pitches. As he dejectedly returned to the dugout, the only vacant seat was next to my father. Babe was no stranger to striking out, so he knew exactly how Lou felt. He tried to lift Lou's spirits: "Never you mind, kid," he boomed. "You'll pickle one next time. You took your cuts anyway. You didn't just stand there and watch the balls go by." Lou was so choked up he didn't even reply. Thus began a very special friendship.

The Yankees won their third consecutive pennant in 1923 and finally dethroned the New York Giants in the World Series after two previous humiliations. In 1924, however, the Yankees failed to win the pennant for the first time in four years, despite another productive season for my father: a league-leading 46 home runs and .378 batting average, coupled with a second consecutive season of good behavior off the field.

The following year told an altogether different story, as Dad reverted to the unrestrained lifestyle of days past, and both he and the Yankees were the worse for it. During the winter of 1924 he abandoned both his diet and his exercise routine, negating the effects of the previous two years in a few short months. He did everything to excess except sleep. Often he would leave the apartment underdressed when there was snow on the ground, with his hair still dripping wet from his shower. By January of 1925 his weight had ballooned to a dangerous 265 pounds, and he regularly suffered from high fevers, stomach cramps and other flu symptoms, all of which he ignored.

By the time Dad reported to St. Petersburg in March for spring training, he was running a 104-degree temperature and suffering from a slight case of pneumonia. Miller Huggins and many of his teammates were gravely concerned about him and felt that he had finally gone too far and pushed his body over the limit. Huggins wanted Dad to rest for a few days and work himself back into shape, but Babe would have none of this "preferential treatment"; instead, he insisted on playing every exhibition game, even one in the rain. Huggins was well aware that Babe was seriously ill. He was also aware of how stubborn Dad could be and the problems that he would create if he took him out of the lineup. Against his better judgment, he left Babe in the line-up and kept his fingers crossed.

Miraculously, Dad led the Yankees in hitting for most of the exhibition tour, which included stops in Birmingham, Alabama, Savannah, Georgia, and Chattanooga and Knox-ville, Tennessee—all traditional stops on the team's way north for the opening of the baseball season. Meanwhile, his condition rapidly deteriorated. Finally, on April 7, my father collapsed as he got off the train in Asheville, North Carolina. When he regained consciousness, he found him-self in a taxi on its way to the Battery Park Hotel, where the team was staying. He complained of dizziness, severe abdominal cramps, and aches and pains throughout his body.

After two days of rest and a brief examination by a local doctor, Babe insisted on returning to New York. He was still a bit wobbly but was able to make it to the train station unassisted. By the time the train reached Washington, Dad was feeling much better, so he celebrated with a large breakfast.

The food and the bumpy train ride were too much for his tender stomach. He ran to the bathroom, where he became violently ill. Once again he was burning up with fever as he splashed cold water on his face, and his weakened legs could no longer support his massive frame. He fainted, smashing his head against the sink as he crumbled to the floor.

Paul Krichell, the Yankee scout who had been monitor-ing Babe's condition on the train, immediately phoned New York and requested that an ambulance meet the train when it reached Penn Station. It was quite a scene. Babe, semi-conscious, was loaded through a window and onto a stretch-er, where he endured a lengthy wait for an ambulance. When it arrived, he was rushed to St. Vincent's Hospital.

After a thorough examination by his personal physician, Dr. Edward King, it was determined that Dad had an in-testinal abscess which would require surgery. Although the ensuing operation was a success, Babe continued to run a fever and lose weight for several weeks afterwards.

Dad's relapse turned out to be far more serious than anyone had expected. Before he was completely recovered, he ended up missing six weeks of the 1925 season. (He only played 96 games the entire season and the critics once again speculated that his career was over.) Despite all the negative publicity generated by Babe's absence from the lineup and a dismal start of the season, the Yankees did experience one boon. Desperately needing to add some punch to his lineup, Miller Huggins summoned Lou Gehrig, a promising, heavy-hitting first baseman, from the minor leagues.

On June 1, 1925, the same day that Babe returned to the Yankee lineup, Miller Huggins called on Gehrig to pinch hit for Pee Wee Wanninger as the Yankees were in the process of losing to the Washington Senators. The diminutive manager had been trying desperately to get Gehrig's bat in the lineup for many months; Lou had torn up the minor leagues in 1924 with his slugging: 40 doubles, 13 triples, 37 home runs, and a .369 batting average, for Hartford of the Eastern League (then Class AA). With Babe out of action for a while, Huggins had his chance; unfortunately, Gehrig did not get a hit. Although the event seemed insignificant at the time, it was the beginning of the greatest endurance record baseball has ever known.

The following day, Wally Pipp, who for many years had been the Yankees regular first baseman, went to Miller Huggins complaining of a headache; he had been hit in the head with a pitched ball and wanted a few days off. Huggins replaced Pipp with Gehrig at first base. Gehrig got three hits and scored a run the next day. Pipp was getting old, and Gehrig simply played too well to merit his removal from the lineup. For fourteen years and 2,130 consecutive games, he remained firmly entrenched in that position, an incredible feat of durability which earned him his nickname, "The Iron Horse."

Over the years, Lou played with spike wounds, bruised ribs, broken fingers, numerous sprains and serious back pain. He always refused to be X-rayed because of the possible consequences: "I would prefer not to know the extent of my injuries," said Gehrig, "so I may keep on playing. If I were X-rayed, they would probably discover that I have a chipped bone or broken finger, which would mean I would have to lay off for a while." More than being obsessed, he loved baseball and would be the first one on the field and the last one to leave. On his off days he would go to Central Park and shag fly balls in dress pants and shoes with the local boys. During his career with New York, the fans could always count on two things: the sun coming up every morning and Lou strolling out to first base.

The fortune of the Yankees changed considerably as Lou Gehrig emerged as an everyday star. In 1926 he drove in 107 runs, had over 100 RBIs for the first of thirteen consecutive years, smashed 47 doubles, and led the league in triples with 20. But, although his numbers were impressive, his awesome home-run power had yet to be realized. Obviously, a man of Gehrig's strength and size was capable of hitting far more than sixteen home runs—something wasn't quite right.

Lou was a "choke" hitter: he grabbed the bat several inches from the end. Under Babe's tutelage, Lou slid his grip down to the end of the bat and began to take a full cut, utilizing all 210 pounds as he attacked each pitch with a vengeance. In addition, Babe redirected Lou's swing. "You've got to learn to hit to right if you're gonna hit home runs," he advised. "You hit to left and center most of the time. Pull your hits to that short right field that most American League parks have, and most of those long putouts, doubles and triples will be home runs."

The time my father spent with Lou paid huge dividends. The following year, 1927, Lou's home-run total soared to 47, and consequently his RBI total ballooned to 175, good enough to lead the league. "Larrapin' Lou" became a full-fledged superstar that year. The heart of the Yankee lineup—Ruth, Gehrig, Tony Lazzeri, Earle Combs and Bob Meusel—became known as "Murderers' Row." On a typical day in Cleveland, Indians third baseman Rube Lutzke was hit on the shoulder and knocked down by one of Babe's screaming line drives. Gehrig followed with a bullet that hit Rube on the shin and cut his legs out from under him. Then, Bob Meusel hit Lutzke with a shot in the stomach. When the inning was over, Lutzke proclaimed, "Why, I would have been safer in a world war!"

In 1927 it was open season once again, as New York's murderous duo staged one of baseball's classic home-run duels. They went neck and neck throughout the year, with Lou usually in the lead by the slimmest of margins. On August 10 Lou was in front, 38-35. By August 25 Babe had evened the score at 40. It looked like there would be a photo finish until September 6, when Babe launched three home runs to take the lead, 47-45. The next day he hit two more, and the home run derby was over. The season ended with Babe setting a new home-run record with 60, while Lou ended with a not-too-shabby 47, a record for teammates that stood until 1961, when Roger Maris and Mickey Mantle hit 61 and 54, respectively.

To give you a better idea of what type of year my father had down the stretch, consider this: In the last 42 games of the season, he hit 25 homers. If he had maintained that pace for an entire year, he would have hit around 90. A stiff challenge always inspired Dad.

In the World Series of 1927, the Yankees faced the National League Champion Pittsburgh Pirates. Miller Huggins decided to have the boys put on a little display of power before the Series actually began. You might call it psychological warfare. "See those bleachers?" asked Huggins. The boys nodded. "I want to see how many of these nice, new, unblemished baseballs you can drop in those stands." As the dumbfounded Pirates looked on, Babe jolted six. Lou was next: five swings, five home runs. No one really knows if that demonstration affected the Pirates, but the Yankees swept the Series in four straight games, a feat they would duplicate in 1928 and 1932 on their way to a record twelve consecutive World Series triumphs.

The following year they put on a hitting display that remains unequaled in World Series history. Babe had ten hits in sixteen at-bats, including three home runs and a Series slugging percentage of .625, all in a four-game Series. Gehrig hit four home runs and knocked in nine runs, while hitting .545. This victory gave the Yankees their third consecutive pennant under Miller Huggins, the second string of three consecutive pennants for the Yankee skipper, the first being 1921-23.

As the twenties neared a close, Babe and Lou were probably the two most popular men in America, and as their popularity grew, so did their friendship. They were bridge partners, fishing buddies, devotees of Mrs. Gehrig's fabulous German cooking and regulars at Army-Navy football games.

Lou would go out of his way to try things that did not appeal to him, just to please Babe, like playing cards into the early morning hours. One of Babe's true passions in life was golf, and for years he had tried to persuade Lou to join him on the links, with no luck. But unbeknownst to my father, Lou started to take private lessons, and before long he was shooting in the low 80s. This came to an end, however, when he found out that golfing had messed up his baseball swing.

By 1928 the barnstorming rule had been recinded, and Babe and Lou's favorite activity became visiting the small, rural towns which had only read of their famous exploits. When Ruth and Gehrig arrived on the scene, there was usually more commotion than when the circus came to town. Babe organized many of the trips and served as their ringleader; it was Babe's "Greatest Show on Earth" that toured the United States. My father would autograph baseballs as he jogged around the bases. On one trip, the players traveled over 8,000 miles from Rhode Island to California, and played for over 200,000 fans.

When Babe and Lou were not on the road, they often spent time in New Rochelle, New York, with Lou's parents, Henry and Christina, affectionately known by Dad—and me as well—as Mom and Pop Gehrig. The Gehrigs loved my father and treated him like a king whenever he was in their home. Mom was a kind, robust German woman, the backbone of the family. The highlight of many evenings was her home-cooked feasts, which were almost as legendary as Babe's home runs. One of the reasons Babe and Mom Gehrig got along so well was because his German was surprisingly good. He did not speak the language fluently, but he could hold his own in a conversation. Pop, on the other hand, suffered from epilepsy and was prone to unpredictable seizures. A quiet man, he habitually took long walks, accompanied by his extraordinary German shepherd, who understood commands in both German and English.

Originally, Mom had objected to Lou becoming a professional ballplayer; she had wanted him to go to college for four years and become an architect. But like everyone else, she was caught up in the excitement of her son's amazing abilities and soon became a permanent fixture at Yankee Stadium. She could regularly be found in her seat behind the New York dugout, although there was one stretch, at the end of the 1927 season, when her smiling face was missing for about two weeks because she was preparing to undergo surgery. Lou was so worried that he went into a prolonged hitting slump because he was unable to concentrate properly.

Mom and Lou saw eye to eye on everything—except women. Lou dated a number of attractive women, but none of them were good enough for him, according to Mom. That all changed when Lou met Eleanor Twitchell, a sophisticated, attractive woman from Chicago. Mom, true to form, was not very enthusiastic about their courtship and tried to convince Lou that he was making a mistake, but Lou had already made up his mind, and in 1934 he proposed.

Mom created a scene the day before the wedding. She and Eleanor got into a tiff about something meaningless, as I remember it, and it upset Eleanor so much that she suggested calling off the wedding. Lou was determined not to let his mother interfere as she had done in the past, so the two got married without Mom Gehrig's blessing. I was only a teenager at the time and did not attend the wedding, but I was told that Mom reluctantly went to the reception and sat unsmiling the entire evening.

My father never forgot the kind treatment he received at the hands of the close-knit Gehrig family. After the Yankees swept the 1928 World Series, someone gave my father a Mexican hairless dog as a present. The next time he saw Mom Gehrig, he was ready. He pulled the dog out of his coat pocket and presented it to her. In turn, she named the chihuahua pup "Jidge," a nickname given to Babe by his teammates.

Mom was very hospitable to the other Yankees as well. After a game, Babe and Lou would be joined by the other members of Murderers' Row for dinner at the Gehrig home in New Rochelle, a short drive from Yankee Stadium. Ruth, Gehrig, Lazzeri, Combs and Meusel might have been famous around the league for their brutal ways with a bat, but once they stepped foot inside the Gehrig home, they were known as "Ma's Boys."

As a young girl, some of my most cherished moments were spent with the Gehrigs, who became my second family. Often I would get to stay for as long as a week at a time, and I always cried when it was time to leave. Mom Gehrig treated me as if I were her own daughter, a refreshing change from Claire's mistreatment. Lou was the only child of four who survived infancy, and I think Mom and I became as close as we did because she loved children and regretted not having a little girl of her own. As for me, I always seemed to be looking for motherly attention, and where better to find it than with Mom Gehrig. We made pies together, went shopping, took the dog for walks, and worked in the garden. I even had my own room, which was bright, cheerful and homey, a far cry from the cubby hole to which I was relegated in the New York apartment.

The Gehrigs came to mean a great deal to me—especially sensitive, handsome Lou, with his wavy hair and dimples. What twelve-year-old girl wouldn't have had a crush on New York's most eligible bachelor, if she was lucky enough to spend as much time with him as I did? I used to sit in the bathroom doorway and watch him shave in the morning before he went to the ballpark. Part of his incredible stamina on the ballfield can be attributed to the constant care he took of his body. He enjoyed his time at home, never smoke or drank, and was usually in bed by ten o'clock.

Prior to the 1928 season, when Lou's contract was up, Babe made him promise not to accept a new contract for a penny less than $30,000 a year. Babe told him, "Don't worry. I know what you're worth." Lou promised, and that seemed to be the end of it.

Lou came out of the salary negotiations in less than an hour, with a broad smile and his head held high. Babe assumed that his plan had worked until a few days later, when he found out that Lou had signed a two-year contract for only $25,000 per year. Babe confronted Lou, demanding to know why he had broken his promise. Gehrig said, "I didn't. I'm going to get more. I got a contract for $50,000, not $30,000." Lou did not want to ruffle any management feathers with excessive contract demands, he just wanted to play ball. It never bothered Lou that Babe made almost ten times as much as he did in 1927--but it bothered Babe!

Babe would hold court before a game with some of the greatest stars of the day—Walter Johnson, Ty Cobb, Tris Speaker—but Lou always preferred to remain in the background. Out of the corner of his eye, Babe would often spot Lou, nervously approaching like a kid wanting an autograph. "When I go to bat, people are still talking about what Ruth had done," said Lou. "If I stood on my head and held the bat in my teeth, none of the fans would pay the slightest attention. But I'm not kicking." Yet, one day at the Stadium, Lou received a thunderous ovation from a special section where some seven hundred kids were seated. Lou turned to Babe and said in amazement, "Gee, Babe, the kids like me."

On a number of occasions, fate's cruel hand snatched away the glory that was rightfully Lou's. For example, in 1931 Lou tied Babe for the home run championship with forty-six, the first year he was on even terms with Babe. Earlier that year, Gehrig had hit a ball that appeared to be a home run into the center field bleachers. Lyn Lary, who was on first base at the time, thought the ball had been caught, so he headed across the infield toward the dugout, thinking the inning was over. Gehrig, running the bases with his head down, never realized what had happened until he was called out for passing Lary on the bases. If not for that unfortunate base-running blunder, Gehrig would have won his first home run title.

Then, on June 2, 1932, Lou smacked four home runs in one game; only a great leaping catch by outfielder Al Simmons prevented him from becoming the only man in history to hit five. Following the game, it was announced that John McGraw, manager of the New York Giants for thirty years, had resigned. Once again Lou received second billing.

When Babe left the Yankees following the 1934 season, it appeared that Lou finally would gain the recognition that had eluded him for so long. But in 1936, along came this rookie. . .Joe DiMaggio.

The Depression had reached its nadir by 1933, and for the first time my father would not escape its harsh sting. Besides a hefty pay cut of $25,000 dollars, other factors contributed to his personal depression. At the age of thirty-nine, Dad's baseball skills had noticeably declined, and Jacob Ruppert had made it clear that Babe's hope of managing the Yankees was a longshot at best. But saddest of all was the misunderstanding that all but ended the close friendship between Babe and Lou.

In 1933 Mom Gehrig made an innocent remark to one of the ballplayers' wives. Tired of seeing me dressed in hand-me-down clothes, she expressed out loud what she had probably been wondering for some time: "Why doesn't Claire dress Dorothy as well as she dresses her own daughter, Julia?" Claire got wind of the remark and told Babe that she wanted nothing to do with the Gehrigs ever again. The next day Babe approached Lou in the locker room and said something about Mom Gehrig having a big mouth. Lou could tolerate a lot of things in life, but insulting Mom Gehrig was not one of them. The battle lines had been drawn.

My world ended when Claire informed me that I would never go to New Rochelle again. After all the Gehrigs had done for me, I wasn't about to stop being friends with them, so whenever I would see the Gehrigs at Yankee Stadium I'd wave to them, even though Claire would be firmly tugging me in the opposite direction.

Babe and Lou would have eventually settled their differences had it not been for Claire, who insisted that Babe never associate with Lou. Claire always felt that Babe was too good for anyone but her. In the end, she succeeded in undermining Babe and Lou's relationship by making Mom Gehrig the scapegoat, when it was her neglectful treatment of me that was really the problem. The two men continued to drift apart, until my father left the picture altogether when he quit the Yankees following the 1934 season.

Some years later, a remark of Babe's was relayed through the newspapers to Lou, whose consecutive-game streak was still going strong. Babe said, "Gehrig ought to quit trying to be an iron man by playing everyday. He'll get a permanent charley horse and fold up all of a sudden." From his home in New Rochelle, Gehrig uncharacteristically lost his temper and fired back, "Mind your own business, Babe!" Both men were irritable at this point in their lives. Babe was frustrated because he felt the owners had alienated him from baseball, and Lou was gradually feeling the tiring effects of a disease that would soon take his life.

In 1938 Lou hit below .300 for the first time since 1925, and the following spring he lost 25 pounds and looked arthritic at first base. He managed only four singles in the first eight games, and concern was growing among the Yankee brass. On May 2, 1939, Lou Gehrig decided the time had come to take himself out of the lineup. After 2,130 consecutive games, 23 grand slams, 1,900 RBIs, and two MVP awards, the durable Dutchman had played his last game. Lou never attempted to pad his streak; he did what he always did—what was best for the team.

May 2, 1939, was a day no Yankee fan or player will ever forget, especially Babe Dahlgren, the man who replaced

Gehrig that day at first base. "Photographers were all over the field," Dahlgren remembered. "They were taking Lou's picture and my picture, then one of Lou and me together.

"Just before Lou was to take the lineup out to home plate, we came face to face in the dugout. I guess every kid yearned for the opportunity I now had, but I can truthfully say that I did not want to play that day. I know there were tears in our eyes as we looked at each other, and I heard myself saying, 'Come on, Lou, you better get out there. You've put me in a terrible spot.' Lou slapped me on the back and said, 'Go on, get out there and knock in some runs.'"

Babe Dahlgren played first base that day and had two hits, including a home run. Gehrig was the first person to greet Dahlgren at home plate. "Gosh, Babe!" he cried. "Why didn't you tell me you felt that way? I would have gotten out of here long ago."

The fact that Gehrig had finally missed a game was a shock, but the news that followed shortly thereafter was heart-wrenching: Gehrig was suffering from amyotrophic lateral sclerosis, a degenerative disease of the nerve cells that control muscular movement. Lou was thirty-six at the time, and his prospects for reaching forty were remote. The Yankees hurriedly arranged for a day to honor their stricken hero. On July 4, 1939, Lou Gehrig had his day at Yankee Stadium, with over 65,000 grief-stricken fans in attendance.

With the game about to begin, there was still no sign of my father. Lou sat in the dugout, nervously monitoring the door, hoping for Babe to arrive. Suddenly, there was a roar from the crowd, and Babe and Claire were shaking hands and waving to the crowd as they made their way to their seats behind the Yankee dugout. Lou's day was now complete. Babe's flair for the dramatic was always a joy to behold, but more importantly he had not disappointed his friend in a time of need. With tears in his eyes, Babe came out of the stands and up to home plate during the ceremonies, instinctively throwing his arms around Lou.

A few moments later, Lou addressed the crowd with one of the most famous and touching speeches in sports history:

". . .They say I've had a bad break, but I have an awful lot to live for. With all this, I consider myself the luckiest man on the face of the earth." Those two memorable lines brought down the house at Yankee Stadium and epitomized the man whom so many people in attendance that day had come to know and love.

During the next two years, Babe often visited Lou in the hospital, even though Claire insisted that he stay away from him. "I'm going to see my friend," he told her, "whether you like it or not."

Everyone prayed for Lou because they realized there was little else they could do. On June 2, 1941, at 10:10 P.M. exactly sixteen years to the day after he started his first game for the Yankees, Lou Gehrig slipped into a coma and died, the victim of an affliction that came to be known as "Lou Gehrig's disease."

9

Banzai, Babu Russu!

In the fall of 1934 Babe took his baseball barnstorming show overseas, to Japan and other parts of the Far East. Connie Mack, the 72-year-old manager of the Philadelphia Athletics, was overseeing the trip, and he selected Babe to manage the club, which was comprised of fifteen players: infielders Lou Gehrig, Charlie Gehringer, Jimmy Foxx, Hal Warstler and Eric McNair; outfielders Babe, Earl Averill, Bing Miller and Lefty O'Doul; pitchers Lefty Gomez, Earl Whitehill, Clint Brown and Joe Cascarella; and catchers Frank Hayes and Moe Berg. Most of the players were accompanied by their wives, as was Babe, who brought along Julia as well. I was left home. Claire insisted that I remain in school, although Julia was whisked in and out of school at a moment's notice. Claire told reporters that Julia, who was seventeen at the time, was given the trip as a graduation present. Well, if that trip was a graduation present, then Julia graduated about fifteen times in five years!

The Japanese eagerly anticipated the celebrated tour of the American all-stars despite the raw political feelings that existed between the two countries due to territorial disputes, oil squabbles and American bans on Japanese immigration; people were more interested in how soon the Americans would arrive and how many home runs they would hit than they were with international relations. As far as the American government was concerned, baseball was not a primary concern; even though the events leading to World War II were well in the future, a wary, mistrustful America had begun to carefully monitor Japan's movement.

Enter Moe Berg. As part of an ingenious undercover plot, Berg doubled as baseball player and spy! As I later read in *Moe Berg: Athlete, Scholar, Spy,* by Louis Kaufman, Barbara Fitzgerald and Tom Sewell, on this very trip Berg was carrying a letter signed by Cordell Hull, Secretary of State under Franklin Delano Roosevelt, which would introduce him to American diplomats.

Why did the United States government choose Moe Berg? For starters, he graduated from Princeton University, studied at the Sorbonne in Paris, received a law degree from Columbia, and was familiar with over ten languages, including Russian, Latin and Japanese. But more importantly, the Japanese trusted Moe. Two years earlier, he had spent many hours teaching the fundamentals of catching to hundreds of athletes at seven Tokyo universities. The Japanese were so impressed with his ability to speak their language that they asked him to join the faculty at Kieo University in Tokyo as a professor of Romance languages. So Moe was the perfect choice.

None of the players had any knowledge of Berg's covert activity, but Joseph Grew, the U.S. ambassador to Tokyo, had been briefed. With Grew's help, Berg gained access to the roof of St. Luke's Hospital in Tokyo, from which he took important photographs of shipping lanes, factories, refineries, train stations, bridges, and numerous other potential targets. Berg's photos made it possible for the military to diagram two significant bombing raids of Tokyo during World War II, the first commanded by Army Air Corps general James Dolittle in 1944 from the aircraft carrier *Hornet*. The authors of the Berg biography also credit Moe's photographs with enabling the U.S. military to plan the 1945 fire bombing of Tokyo.

Moe became the ultimate tourist, traveling around Japan and taking photographs of its various cultural, geological and sociological attributes—the Great Buddha of Kamakura, Mount Fuji, rice paddies, school children at play, traditional aspects of Japanese life—anything that might "catch his eye." Dozens of people followed Moe, Babe and the other all-stars around the city, stopping them for autographs and pictures. It was a comical sight: Babe and Moe, at six feet, towered over the crowd of admirers.

Berg's camera followed him everywhere, even to formal dinner parties and speaking engagements. It got to the point that it looked suspicious if Moe did *not* have his camera with him. By reading Japanese literature, carrying around daily newspapers, and conversing with villagers and lecturing statesmen and politicians, he was able to blend in to society. This chameleon-like quality was reinforced by the fact that the Japanese people were pleased and flattered because he was so impressed by their culture; it was rare that one of the revered American athletes took more than a passing interest in their country.

Moe even showed his "amateur" movies in the presence of representatives of the news media to further his tourist stance. But the Japanese government finally caught on. The secret police stopped a game in progress to escort Berg off the field. They searched him in the clubhouse but came up empty-handed.

Before Babe was allowed to return home, he was ordered to forward all his film to the Japanese authorities. When they finally sent Babe's film back, all areas where key installations might have existed had been blacked out. No explanation was given, but the fact that Moe and Babe were close friends and spent a great deal of time together in Japan must have aroused suspicion. In fact, Moe was the only player Babe trusted to escort Julia, of whom Babe was very protective, to dinners and on tours of the city.

Berg continued his espionage activities during World War II, eventually discovering the identities and whereabouts of Hitler's leading scientists and, in turn, the extent of Germany's progress toward building an atomic bomb. Albert Einstein once said to Moe, "If you teach me about baseball, I'll teach you about the atomic bomb."

But in Japan of 1934, the name of the game was baseball, American-style. When the American all-stars arrived, they were greeted by a welcome party of photographers and newspapermen aboard their ship, the *Empress of Japan*. A frenzied crowd of well-wishers besieged Babe in his room for autographs and pictures. After enduring almost three hours, Babe jokingly told photographers that he thought he would go blind from the flashbulbs.

Babe took time out from the festivities to emphasize the importance of the games to be played and the fact that his team of all-stars intended to win every game. "We're dead serious about this trip," said Babe. "It isn't a joyride. We've come to play ball."

The following day a parade was given in honor of the famed foreigners which shook the very foundation of Tokyo. As the procession began, thousands of delirious fans cheered, "*Banzai*, Babe Ruth! *Banzai*, Lou Gehrig! *Banzai*, Jimmy Foxx!" *Banzai* translates, "May you live ten thousand years." Before long, the police were unable to control the wild crowd, which was reported to exceed 800,000 persons in the Ginza district alone, an area equivalent to Broadway in New York. Anxious autograph-seekers jumped on the fenders of cars and begged for their heroes to sign anything, even parts of their anatomy. People threw presents and bouquets of flowers into the players' laps. Babe waved a Japanese flag in one hand and an American flag in the other, as the Toyama Military Band played the *Kimigayo*, Japan's national anthem, and *Stars and Stripes Forever*.

The Americans were the toast of Tokyo. The parade lasted over an hour and brought the city to a standstill, one of the most incredible displays of public emotion in the history of Tokyo.

Later that evening, in the Hibiya Amphitheater, the leaders of Japan formally welcomed their celebrated guests. Babe was introduced last and quite naturally received the longest and most vociferous ovation. As a fitting close to a memorable day, Babe directed his remarks to the wonderful people of Japan, who had received him and his teammates with open arms. "We had come expecting a welcome from you, but we did not expect the welcome to be of such magnitude," he said. "Speaking for the members of my party, may I say that each and every one of us will never forget, as long as we live, the warm reception you have given us. I thank you from the bottom of my heart."

The sixty thousand tickets for the opening game in Tokyo's Meiji Shrine Park had sold out three weeks in advance. Undaunted by the slim odds, thousands of fans drove hundreds of miles and camped out for as long as three days, hoping to find a ticket. During batting practice, the Americans put on quite a power display, depositing a number of treasured souvenirs in the distant stands; hitting the long ball in Japan was far more difficult than in the United States because of the huge dimensions of the Japanese ballparks. On the previous barnstorming trip, in 1931, no American hit a home run at Meiji Shrine Park. In fact, any player who even reached the wall was honored by having his name and the date of the clout painted under a circle where the ball hit the fence.

Babe was not the home run hitter in 1934 that he was during his heyday, but the fans still expected a home run every time he came to bat—Babe's age and the distance of the fence were of no concern to the Japanese faithful.

He failed to hit a home run in the first game, won by the Americans, 17-1; he walked three times and had one hit in six at-bats. Throughout the game, impatient fans screamed at the local pitcher to give Babe and his teammates fatter pitches to hit.

In the second game, won by the Americans, 5-1, Babe hit two towering fly-ball outs to right field, both of which would easily have been home runs in any American League ballpark. The fans were again disappointed, but Babe kept them entertained by clowning around at first base.

At a party that evening, Dad shared a universal message with the youth of Japan: "Baseball players are not born. Practice makes perfect, no matter what sport it might be— tennis, golf, swimming or any other," he said. "Having a ball and a glove mean nothing. The idea is, you have to hustle and practice and think baseball day and night to become a great star. For myself, I have been playing this game since I was six years old. So the Japanese youngsters who wish to be future Gehrigs and Gehringers must play the game hard and love to play it. We must love to do anything we want to do well."

After a drought of four games without a round-tripper, Babe finally found the bleachers in the fifth game, much to the delight of sixty thousand cheering fans. He received a four-minute standing ovation, which he gratefully acknowledged by bowing his head and tipping his hat. Babe's first-inning home run provided Lefty Gomez with the margin of victory, as my favorite southpaw struck out nineteen batters en route to a 10-0 shutout.

While traveling by train to some of the smaller cities, such as Hakodate, Sendai and Toyama, Babe's barnstormers encountered some unforeseen complications. Many of the allstars had to sleep with their legs dangling over the side of their berths, because men over six feet tall in the Orient were quite rare.

Even though the Americans remained undefeated throughout the tour, the real emphasis was not on winning but on the true spirit of sportsmanship and competition. In one game, after a ball had gone through my father's legs, he retrieved it and playfully threw it into the crowd.

Babe finished the seventeen-game tour with a teamleading thirteen home runs, all of which came in the last thirteen games. And in typical Ruth fashion, America's goodwill ambassador said farewell to the Tokyo fans with a grand-slam.

Although the American sluggers dominated most of the contests, the Japanese players felt that each game was a learning experience and that they were improving every day. They were obsessed with "the grand old game" and believed that baseball was as much their national pastime as ours. Their ultimate goal was to one day participate in a true "World" Series.

Japan at the time was highly competitive in most of the international sports like swimming, track and golf, but was still sub-par in baseball, the favorite sport of millions of Japanese. To further their education, the Japanese sent many of their leading college coaches to study American methods of strategy and conditioning, but what they really wanted was a full-time resident instructor. They approached Dad.

The Japanese were in awe of Babe and felt that, if they could convince him to remain indefinitely in Japan to teach them baseball, the possibilities were endless. They affectionately tried to bribe him into staying by offering the lifestyle of a king, including a huge salary, maids, chauffeurs, houses, and anything else his heart desired. Babe declined their generous offer because of his many obligations back home and the fervent patriotism he felt toward his country.

One sad footnote: Shortly after the American all-stars left Japan, Masutaro Shoriki, the Tokyo newspaper publisher most responsible for bringing the American team to Japan, was stabbed to death by a member of the Secret Warlike Gods Society. Obviously the fanatic nationalists resented the publisher's—and the public's—admiration and praise for Babe and his touring all-stars; such wild displays of emotion should have been reserved for military heroes or Emperor Hirohito.

My father felt betrayed by the Japanese when they bombed Pearl Harbor. When the news came over the radio in his apartment at 173 West 89th Street, he bellowed, "Why, those sneaky bastards! I'll give them *banzai!*" My father immediately declared his own war on Japan. He stormed around the apartment, cursing loudly and grabbing anything Japanese that caught his eye. Angrily, he headed for the nearest window—and it was bombs away. He ripped down a beautiful, hand-embroidered, custom-framed Japanese flag and broke it over his knee; the last I saw of it, it was sailing up 89th Street toward Central Park.

It was total pandemonium. I ran just ahead of him grabbing and hiding what I could. I had to duck to avoid being hit in the face with an Oriental doll that was headed fifteen stories to the pavement. He then took a priceless, antique bronze urn which the Japanese had given to him as a trophy and violently flung it against the doorjamb. I have that urn in my living room today, and it still has the dent, a constant reminder to me of his fury. All I know is, my father brought me back a kimono, and I'm glad I wasn't wearing it at the time!

During World War II Babe's impact on the Japanese became even more evident. In April 1944 Japanese soldiers attempted to storm the United States Marine lines on Cape Gloucester, New Britain, with the battle cry, "To hell with Babe Ruth"; they felt no malice toward him personally, only the American ideals he represented. My father doubled his efforts with the Red Cross after hearing that remark. Ironically, the American military used "Babe Ruth" as one of its passwords, because the Japanese had great difficulty pronouncing the letter *R*. Earlier evidence of that fact occured in 1931, when a group of American all-stars toured Japan. Lefty Grove, a thirty-one game winner with the Philadelphia Athletics that year, once struck out six consecutive Japanese batters on nineteen pitches, only to be hailed by adoring fans as "Glove! Glove! Glove!"

The Japanese were deeply saddened when they received word of Babe's death in 1948; in his memory, according to the *Sporting News*, "[e]very ballgame in the country was halted for one minute in silent tribute to baseball's home run champion, known in the Land of the Rising Sun as *'Babu Russu.'*"

10

The Last Straw

I wasn't allowed to date until my junior year in high school—Claire's rule—which made me feel very left out, because most of my friends were already dating and attending proms. When I could finally go out, my father met my boyfriends at the door when they came to pick me up and always reminded me not to stay out too late. My curfew was midnight, but I always came in at 12:05 A.M., just to antagonize Claire.

After all these years, I was sick of being Claire's punching bag, so whenever the opportunity presented itself, I joyfully rebelled. I began by sneaking out of the apartment late at night to see my boyfriends, after Dad and Claire had gone to bed. My bedroom was to the left of the front door, and all the other bedrooms were to the right, so it was almost impossible for Claire to hear me leaving, and since I didn't have to worry about her tucking me in at night, my escape was foolproof.

The elevator would be too conspicuous, so I had to walk down fifteen flights of stairs—which really kept me in good shape. When I returned at 2:00 A.M. or so, the doormen always gave me puzzled looks, but I had to face them because I was too tired to walk up the stairs. They must have thought my behavior was funny because they never said a word to Claire.

After that I started playing hooky from school, once for two straight weeks; I used my carfare and lunch money to buy tickets to see Glenn Miller and Tommy Dorsey perform with their bands at the Paramount Theater. After about a week of coming home as if everything was normal, Babe asked me, "How's school these days?"

I shrugged my shoulders and answered confidently, "Fine."

My father looked at me sternly, knowing full well that I was lying, and said, "Is that so?" Raising his voice slightly, he said, "Well, it probably would be fine if you had been there for the past week." I had obviously overlooked the fact that the truant officer was calling every day looking for me. My truancy must have brought back unhappy memories of my father's own days of regularly missing school.

I was confined to my room again, this time for a month. The following week my father enrolled me in Robert Louis Stevenson private school. I was awarded an art scholarship which reduced the tuition considerably; no doubt this appealed to Claire's penny-pinching ways. In fact, I was shocked that Claire was actually allowing me to attend private school; in most cases when she knew I wanted something, she would go out of her way to see that I didn't get it. In the back of my mind I wondered, "Could my father have gone to bat for me?"

As time passed I got bolder and more vindictive, roller-skating in the apartment, playing the "sacred" piano—which I was only allowed to look at—with my friend Carolyn, and using Claire's charge account to buy clothes at Bergdorf-Goodman.

When I was sixteen I joined my father on a barnstorming trip to South Bend, Indiana. While there he had the use of a chauffeur-driven limousine. One day I told the chauffeur that I knew how to drive, when in fact I had never been behind the wheel of a car, and then proceeded to side-swipe a parked car. It was only a small dent, so the chauffeur and I decided to keep it a secret—after all, it was such a big car and the dent was so small, who would notice? Obviously the owner of the car did, because shortly after we returned to New York, Dad received a bill, along with a letter explaining what had happened.

Shortly thereafter, my father approached me and asked me if I would like to learn how to drive.

I looked at him suspiciously. "Sure. Why?"

He responded, "Because I think I'd be a better teacher than the chauffeur, who, by the way, no longer has a job."

As I reached my senior year, Claire still had me wearing short dresses and knee socks. I was seventeen years old and had never worn a pair of nylon stockings. I knew I looked ridiculous, but Claire insisted on dressing me. "You won't look good in stockings," she said. The very first pair of high heels I had were an old, beat-up pair of Claire's that no longer fit. She thought she was doing me a favor by letting me wear what was not good enough for her. I got Julia's old dresses, too. Julia had gained a bit of weight over the years. What a sight I was, weighing 115 pounds and wearing dresses that were made for a 198-pound woman!

In high school I was told I had a lot of talent as a fashion designer and was even offered scholarships to Columbia University and the Traphagen School of Design. Unfortunately, I never ended up going to college, because Claire convinced Dad that "The Ruths don't accept charity." Besides, Julia didn't want to go to college, and Claire had no intention of letting me show up her daughter. Claire's favoritism toward Julia was something with which I would have to live for my entire life; Babe, however, treated Julia and me equally. In fact, when Julia was hospitalized in 1938 with a growth on the side of her neck, my father gladly volunteered for a blood transfusion which helped save her life.

I anxiously awaited my eighteenth birthday. Turning eighteen meant one thing to me—freedom. I really could not tolerate living at home anymore. Each day grew more and more unbearable. Even Christmas, the one day of the year to which I looked forward, had become just the same as the rest. My childhood memories of my father bringing home our Christmas tree were all but forgotten. We decorated the tree without him, because he would be out visiting the sick in hospitals and would not return until late at night, exhausted. By the late 1930s I was lucky if I got a ten-dollar gold piece in the palm of my hand for Christmas. It's not that I didn't appreciate the gold piece, it's just that it was given so half-heartedly that I would rather have received nothing. I was used to receiving sentimental gifts, such as lifesize dolls, pedal cars or stuffed animals. However small or large, they were always gifts from the heart.

The last straw came in 1939. Dad had surprised me one day by bringing home a puppy. Without my knowledge, Claire took the dog to the veterinarian to be spayed. The operation was not successful, and the dog died. When she told me about the horrible incident, I picked up a heavy ashtray and hurled it at her, missing her head by only a couple of inches and leaving a huge hole in the wall. My father just sat there and acted as if nothing had happened.

Neither Babe nor Claire were very surprised when I left home shortly after my eighteenth birthday. I didn't leave in a rage as I had so often done before; rather, I left quietly, without telling either of them where I was going and without taking my belongings. It was a small victory but a victory nonetheless to have finally mustered up enough courage to walk out.

One part of me felt scared, not knowing what to expect, but another part felt relieved and looked forward to finally having some control over my own destiny. I had mixed emotions about my father. I felt sorry for him because he had spent so much of his life trying to help other people, and I really believed that he had ended up with the short end of the stick because his home life was so miserable. His public was more his "family" than his real family ever was. Interacting with the public in a personal way made him happier than just about anything else. He enjoyed being a star but did not let his stardom prevent him from rolling up his sleeves and mingling with the likes of anybody.

The most important ingredient missing from his recipe for true happiness was love. In a way it was his own fault. He allowed himself to be a victim. As I planned to leave, I wondered if Babe and I would ever have a chance to sit down and have that intimate conversation between father and daughter that I had always craved; I wasn't optimistic, but I looked forward to the day nonetheless. I loved Dad very much and felt sorry for any unnecessary heartache I might have caused him. I prayed he would understand why I had to leave, and that he would find it in his heart to forgive me.

Looking back on the day I left home, I remember crying as I said goodbye to Claire's mother, Carrie, who was the only one home in the apartment at the time. I owed her so much for the love, guidance and attention she had given me during the past ten years. Without Carrie, I would have been forced to leave long ago. She was a dear friend who taught me how to cook, sew and crochet, and how best to prepare myself for the future. She knew that I was badly mistreated and tried whenever possible to take my side in an argument. She would also ask Claire for money, which she would secretly give to me.

As a child I was punished for leaving my room in the middle of the night to sleep in Carrie's room, which I did because my room was isolated from the rest of the bedrooms and the howling courtyard winds would often frighten me. The void that Carrie filled in my life was an important one. She was like a mother to me. In the end, Carrie knew how I felt about her and understood why I had to leave, so we said a peaceful goodbye.

Walking toward the front door, I turned and paused briefly. As I slowly looked around the spacious apartment, little was of any significance to me, until I focused on a wall in the hallway, filled with dozens of pictures of my father, smiling and clowning as he so often did with many of the stars of the day. There he was with Ty Cobb, Rogers Hornsby, Tris Speaker, George Sisler, Walter Johnson, Lou Gehrig and many, many others.

For that one moment, all was tranquil. What a refreshing change from the usual turbulence! I reflected over the years and could hear a few of Claire's painful "reminders" repeating like a broken record: "Julia would never do that...No! You're not allowed!...I can't wait to be alone!...Julia would never do that...No! You're not allowed!...I can't wait to be alone..."

As I closed the front door firmly and began to walk away, I wondered if my father could be far behind.

11

Has Anybody Seen Babe Ruth?

As the years went by, Claire developed a serious drinking problem. My father spent less time at home, and Claire spent more time with the bottle. Although she was blatantly intoxicated morning, noon and night, I never remember her having a hangover. Some days she even started the day with gin in her milk or soda!

Not only were her mental capacities for anything but baseball statistics and money slipping, but also her once lush beauty was rapidly deteriorating. Yet, though she was miserable and made all of us around her miserable, it was still sad to stand by and watch this happen. My father and Claire had only been married for seven years, but she looked as though twenty horrendous years had passed. In her younger days, Claire could look terrific when she rolled out of bed in the morning; now she was overweight, wan, and desperately in need of help to pull herself back together again.

As a result, Claire did not always behave herself in public. I remember one awful incident which occurred at Yankee Stadium after my father had passed away. She had gotten so drunk in a restaurant before the game that an usher and a friend, one on each side, had to carry her out of the ballpark—chair and all.

My father was constantly pleading with her to stop drinking, but she always refused. The two had brutal arguments: "You've ruined every friendship I've ever had," he would yell, to which Claire would accuse, "You'd be nowhere without me."

Although he was greatly depressed, Babe's flamboyant personality and extraordinary baseball skills continued to touch millions of people all around the world. He never allowed his fans to glimpse the dark, tormented side of his life because he did not want his personal problems with Claire to taint his public image.

Soon Dad got tired of coming home to a wife who was usually sitting dead drunk in a chair. He relied on excuses, whenever possible, to get away from the apartment, and when the excuses failed, there was always hunting, fishing or golfing. He played golf in such frigid temperatures that it was often necessary to use his golf club to hammer the tee into the frozen ground.

Often he would tell Claire that he was going hunting or fishing, when in reality he was off to spend a weekend with the boys. I'm not sure where he went, but I know he wasn't hunting or fishing. To make his story look good, he wouldn't shave for three days; then, just before returning, he would buy whatever it was he was supposed to be after. One of his hunting trips that I remember left from Grand Central Terminal and barely made it as far as the New York suburb of Westchester. When the proud "hunting party" returned, a hefty load of venison was strapped to the roof of the train. After a "fishing trip," he secretly would buy a dozen of whatever kind of fish was available at that time of year from the Washington Market. He would come in the door with a big smile on his face, dump the sack of fish on the kitchen table, and proudly say, "Look what I caught!" That clever ploy worked until the day that he dumped out the fish and discovered that the market had individually wrapped each of his "catches" in butcher paper. That took a bit of explaining!

However, most of my father's hunting expeditions were legitimate. I know, because I was the one who spent many a late night plucking his feathered trophies—mostly quails, pheasants and ducks. It got to the point that I never wanted to see another duck as long as I lived. In fact, shortly after I remarried, my second husband surprised me with two freshly killed pheasants. I was furious. I had no intention of plucking them. Instead, I opened the freezer door and threw the birds, feathers and all, into the back, where they stuck and remained until the day we threw out the refrigerator.

My father loved spending time in the country and took his authentic hunting trips quite seriously, which would come as no surprise to anyone who ever competed against him in any sport, from bowling to shuffleboard. It never mattered if he was only playing a friendly game of cards; if he was losing, chances were he would not let his opponent go to bed until he got even.

Babe hunted and fished regularly, mostly in New York, New Jersey and Pennsylvania. He usually went with a number of retired ballplayers, including "Smokey" Joe Wood, his old teammate with the Boston Red Sox. However, his favorite party consisted of three pitchers: Harry Harper, Russ Van Atta and Johnny Vander Meer. Maybe it was only appropriate that all four were lefthanders. Harper pitched for the Yankees in 1921 and Van Atta pitched for them in 1933 and 1934. Vander Meer was best known for being the only pitcher in baseball history to hurl two consecutive no-hitters. My father first met Johnny in 1938, on the night he pitched his second no-hitter against the Brooklyn Dodgers at Ebbets Field, but the two did not become friends until the winter after that season. Johnny, the only surviving member of the foursome, vividly recalled some of their more memorable hunting and fishing escapades.

"Whenever we went duck hunting, I would shoot first and usually miss, then the Babe would shoot second and hit. He was an outstanding guy with a shotgun.

"The night before duck hunting, it was important to get to bed early, because wake-up call was at 5:00 A.M. Most guys liked to get seven or eight hours' sleep. Not Babe. All he needed was two or three. So this one particular time we all went to bed early, while Babe went out to visit some friends in the area. There wasn't anyplace the Babe didn't know somebody.

"Well, around 2:00 A.M. he comes back, turns on all the lights, makes plenty of noise, and wakes everybody up. 'Nobody goes to sleep the night before duck hunting,' he said. He wouldn't let any of us go back to sleep, and for the next three hours, we all just sat there in our pajamas.

"Another time we went duck hunting right before the war. It was the first year in quite some time that you were allowed to shoot the Brandt, a small goose that comes from Greenland. The geese were protected, so you were only allowed two each. I'd shoot at them damn things all day and hit only one. The Babe never had any problems the way I did. He was one hell of a shot.

"He used to call me 'Lefthander' and Van Atta 'Red Ass.' Between Van Atta and Babe you had two pretty good pranksters. One night Van Atta invited the Babe to Newton, New Jersey, for a big sportsmen's dinner. We all knew what he had in store for Babe.

"Van Atta tied this big barnyard turkey to the ground behind a hill. The next morning, as we approached that hill, someone yelled, 'Babe! There's one!' Babe then snuck up from behind and shot that turkey. He didn't know a thing about it until that night, when we all had a good laugh at his expense. When you pulled a prank on him, I can guarantee you one thing, he was gonna get even with you one way or another. His favorite saying was 'I've got to get even with that guy.'

"The following year, Babe received a fine hunting dog as a present and decided to give it to Van Atta. 'I've got a good dog for ya,' he said. Van Atta was very pleased with the dog's performance and decided to keep him. As soon as he started driving home, the dog got carsick and threw up all over his brand new Cadillac. So Babe got even for the turkey incident.

"No matter where we went, Babe was a very photographic individual. When he walked in a place, everyone knew he was the Babe. He and President Roosevelt were probably the only two guys who couldn't hide. He was a fun guy. He raised a little hell, but I never saw him offend anyone."

From the late 1930s until shortly before his death in 1948, my father's favorite hideaway was Greenwood Lake, an affluent, predominantly German resort area about fifty miles northwest of New York City in Orange County, New York. Greenwood Lake was rustic and quiet, ideal for outdoor sports like hunting, fishing, boating, skiing and tobogganing. It was a perfect spot for vacationing movie stars and show people who wanted to avoid publicity. My father was able to unwind, forget about baseball, and leave his marital problems behind. Amazingly enough, he went there over a period of nearly ten years, yet no one ever remembered seeing Claire with him.

Occasionally I joined him at Greenwood Lake, but for the most part he went by himself. Dad and I had reluctantly drifted apart after my marriage, and I'm not sure who was to blame. I had my hands full with three children and a husband who didn't make life any easier, and Dad was at his wits' end with Claire's tirades.

I thought about him often, knowing how unhappy he was, but there was very little I could do about his situation. When I called him, Claire usually answered and informed me that she had absolutely no idea where he was or when he was coming home—and I knew first-hand that Dad could certainly be elusive when he wanted to be. The thought had crossed my mind on more than one occasion that to accurately keep track of Babe's whereabouts, someone would have to tag him with a radio transmitter, as if he belonged to some endangered species.

As a more feasible alternative, his friends and acquaintances from the time he spent at Greenwood Lake shared some of their favorite stories with me. Mainly I was curious whether his personality had changed during this period of his life, when he and I had for the most part lost contact. After talking with those who knew him best from his days spent at the lake, I was happily convinced that, from all indications, Babe was still Babe.

When he first discovered Greenwood Lake, Babe rented a "shack" in Sterling Forest, an area a few miles from the center of town. But as he became more comfortable with the people, he moved closer to the water and stayed in a small cottage on the grounds of Greck's Maplewood Inn, which was situated right on the lake. Greck's became his preferred hangout, and Teddy Greck, the owner's fourteen-year-old son, became one of his favorite sidekicks. This was around 1945-46. Babe was a lonely man at this point in his life, and he was not looking for an intimate relationship with a woman; instead he needed some simple companionship. Teddy was like a little brother to him. Babe would pick him up from school and take him hunting, fishing and boating. The two of them really enjoyed each other's company and could frequently be found wrestling on the cottage floor in their pajamas.

"Once in a while Babe would make an appearance at the schoolyard and hit a few," Teddy told me. "And believe me, he could still wallop them. Back in those days we only had one ball, if we were lucky, and Babe would come up to bat and hit the thing a mile into the lake. Then he'd drop the bat and start walking away. 'Okay boys!' he'd say, 'That's enough baseball. Let's go for a boat ride.'

"He had a flashy, five-thousand-dollar speedboat which was really something, and he'd take us around the lake to all the different taverns. He'd have a shot in his beer and we'd have cokes. Other times we'd go hunting and all he'd wear was an undershirt, a big fur coat, coonskin hat and a pair of boots. That was about it."

"One trick he taught me with a shotgun was how to shoot underneath a can and then shoot it a second time as it flew through the air. On weekends he'd wake up in the morning and say, 'Hey, boy! Let's go ice fishing.' He'd give me ten dollars for bait, which was a ridiculous amount of money, and then go back to sleep. 'Wake me when you get back, boy!,' he'd say. Then he'd cook me breakfast; his specialty was "The Hole-in-one." He would cut out the middle of a piece of toast, put an egg in the middle and fry it.

"I'll always remember Babe as a guy who was carefree and happy-go-lucky," said Teddy. "When I think of him, I think of that big smile of his that could make you melt."

Dad was famous for leaving lasting impressions. Wilburt Christman, historian and one-time mayor of Greenwood Lake, will never forget the first time he saw my father. "I was standing on the corner in the center of town when I looked up and saw someone back this brand-new Pierce Arrow into a tree," Christman said with a hearty chuckle. "Who gets out of the car but Babe Ruth. He went around to look at the big dent in the middle of the trunk, grumbled to himself, jumped back into the car and drove off. He was quite a sight with that big fur coat down to his knees. He looked like a gigantic bear."

As you might expect, Babe was the center of attention in Greenwood Lake, but as the people grew accustomed to his presence they accepted him as part of their community and respected his desire for privacy.

Greenwood Lake was surrounded by taverns and restaurants, and my father was no stranger to any of them. "He was known to bounce around from bar to bar for a night on the town without any money," recalled Jack Demarest, owner of the Demarest Lodge and an old drinking buddy of Dad's. "Babe's credit was good everywhere he went, because the following weekend he would make the rounds and pay everyone whatever he owed." Some of his favorite haunts were Herbert and Gertrude's, the High Spot, the Old Hidelberg, the Continental, Demarest's Lodge and, of course, Greck's Maplewood Inn.

One afternoon, Wilburt Christman told me, Babe was sitting in Greck's when a man came inside looking for one-dollar donations for the local Boy Scout troop; they were building a new headquarters and needed money for supplies. After the man had collected money from the entire bar, he approached Babe, who said, "Count up all the money and whatever it is, I'll match it."

Gordon Livingston, a long-time friend of Dad's and the owner of the High Spot, bet him that he could not drive a golfball across the lake. My father won the bet in a most unusual manner. He slyly waited until winter and then drove the ball across the lake when it was frozen. Because of the ice, the ball kept rolling until it reached the other side!

Another proprietor remembered my father sitting at the corner of the bar, pouring his own drinks with a bottle of scotch he had brought with him. Still another recalled Babe leading singalongs, using a lamp as a microphone.

"Babe came to Greenwood Lake to get away from all the handshaking, and to try and relax," said Demarest. "But once he got started, he didn't do much relaxing. I might see Babe one weekend and then not hear from him for six weeks, but then that's the way Babe was. He didn't get overly friendly with many people, but he was still well liked. He wasn't the easiest guy in the world to figure out, but after a while I felt I understood him pretty well. We got along because I didn't ask him a million questions or treat him like a celebrity. When my mother was sick, he gave me an autographed picture of himself which really cheered her up."

There was always a soft spot in Dad's heart for worthy causes. Sometimes he would be in the middle of dinner at Greck's when a group of boys would come running over to his table and ask him to go outside to pose for a photograph with them. Even though it was an imposition, Babe would never say no. Dad and his "boys" were as natural together as hot dogs with mustard. When he went tobogganing, he paid the neighborhood boys twenty-five cents to help tow him up the mountain. And when he grew tired of that, he would take them over to the Long Pond Inn to watch boxers like Joe Louis, "Stonewall" Jackson, Ray Robinson and Tippy Larkin train.

The legend of Babe Ruth survives today in the hamlet of Greenwood Lake, much the same as it does in many other cities and towns where he stopped long enough to give the people something to talk about. During World War II my father played an active role in Greenwood Lake's Thoughts from Home, a monthly charity drive which sent care packages to the men overseas. The packages contained shaving cream, razors, combs, homemade cookies, knitted socks, writing paper, deodorant, and other necessities. Dad contributed autographed baseballs and pictures from his friends in the major leagues. The women who organized Thoughts from Home were so grateful to my father for his support that they erected a plaque in his honor that still stands in Greenwood Lake.

Unfortunately, when my father returned home, I became the main target of Claire's cruel, intoxicated verbal abuse. Although she never laid a hand on me, the torture she inflicted had a deep psychological effect. Domestic squabbles were constantly taking place in one form or another; it was hard to believe that we could not live peaceably in an eleven-room apartment. During one of Claire's nastier tirades, she called me a guttersnipe. I returned the compliment by calling her a whore. My father overheard me and was shocked; he told me not to use that type of language. I told him what she had called me and stormed out of the room, while Dad began arguing with Claire.

As the argument continued, I suddenly got the courage, in the midst of all the emotion, to ask Babe if I was his real daughter. You see, Claire always introduced me as "our adopted daughter," and always insinuated that I was an orphan. Over the years, she succeeded in casting doubt in my mind, as well as in the minds of others. Although I *was* Claire's adopted daughter, I am my father's flesh and blood. That fact, I'm sure, was a continuing thorn in her side—it was the one thing that she could never take away from me.

His eyes watered and his face turned bright red. Painfully he answered, "Damn it, yes!" He stormed out of the room before I could ask him the most important question: Who was my real mother? The answer would not come until much later—nearly forty-five years later, as a matter of fact.

Claire did her devious and malicious best to exclude me from any and all family functions. Whenever we had dinner guests, she sent me into the kitchen to eat alone. "Not with the grownups" was her standard reasoning.

I lay awake nights, unable to fall asleep. Sometimes I passed the time by writing hate letters to Claire, but I always tore them up before she could find them.

Our Riverside Drive apartment became the late-night hangout for sportswriters, celebrities, and show people. Sportswriter Ed Sullivan, bandleader Vincent Lopez, cartoonist Billy DeBeck, composer Peter DeRose, and many others frequently dropped by.

One couple who visited quite often was Charlie Ellias and his wife, Juanita, both close friends of my father. At the time, I had no idea how important a role they were to play in my adult life.

Charlie Ellias was the head accountant for Harry M. Stevens, the famed ballpark and racetrack concessionaire, and a man who my father trusted like a brother. Charlie had a brilliant mind for business, and Dad usually consulted him before signing any contract. In 1929 my father was earning $70,000 with the Yankees and even more from endorsements, public appearances, ghost-written newspaper articles and miscellaneous investments; he had so much going on that he probably could have employed a team of accountants to keep track of his finances. Although Claire wanted to supervise all his money matters, my father sought Charlie's advice without her knowledge.

Charlie was one of my favorite people, a rare individual who treated me like gold whenever I visited his office at Yankee Stadium, which was owned by his boss. He would always greet me with a big smile and an even bigger scoop of ice cream, and he used to let me shake the coin boxes from the vendors, separating all the change. Claire told me to stay away from Charlie because I was a nuisance, but I ignored her. Pretending to go to the bathroom, I would sneak into his office.

My father was responsible for introducing Charlie to Juanita Jennings, who, incidentally, had been one of my father's old flames. Juanita was an attractive, dark-haired beauty of Mexican descent. Her grandfather was Don Francisco Madera, the colorful president of Mexico from 1911 to 1913, when he met an untimely death at the hands of assassins. Juanita had olive skin, bewitching green eyes, and a fiery temper. She could be vain and stubborn, but Charlie catered to her every whim and thoroughly enjoyed spoiling her. In 1929, not long after their introduction, Charlie and Juanita were married. Charlie's Jewish family promptly disowned him for marrying a Christian girl.

The two couples became very close over the years. Curiously, Claire and Juanita became the best of friends, even though their personalities were worlds apart. I'm sure that Claire did not know that Juanita and my father had once dated, because if she had, I doubt that Juanita would have been the only woman she trusted around him. As it was, Juanita posed no threat to her.

Babe Ruth and family setting sail for Bermuda, 1933. (photo courtesy National Baseball Library, Cooperstown, NY)

Dad and I in the late 1930s. He was on his way to Florida for spring training. (photo courtesy National Baseball Library, Cooperstown, NY)

Playing at his second love in Florida.

My father at Greenwood Lake in his beloved boat.

Babe and some hunting buddies after a successful trip. I have the mounted head of the deer on the right hanging on my wall—Dad was very proud of it.

Juanita Jennings Ellias—notice that Helen's dinner ring is now on her finger.

*Juanita, Babe and Claire at a New Jersey wrestling match
right after Dad retired. Charlie Ellias is in the next row
wearing the sunglasses.*

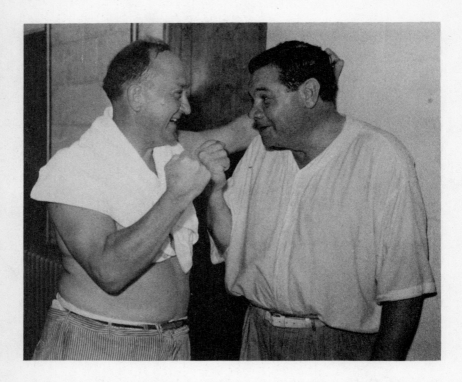

Ty Cobb and Babe Ruth, two of the greatest baseball players of all time.

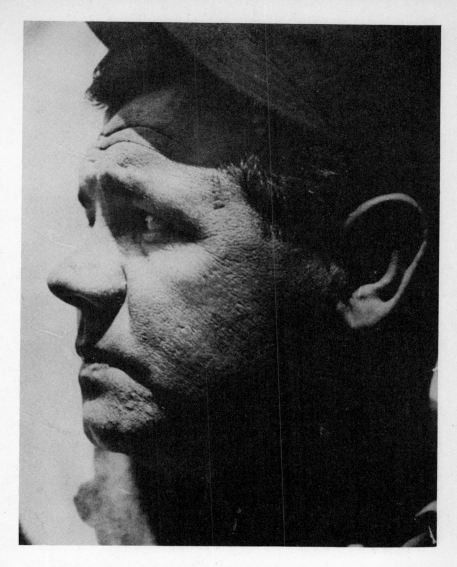

One of my favorite pictures of my father, taken around 1935. This study says a lot. (photo by J. Anthony Lopez)

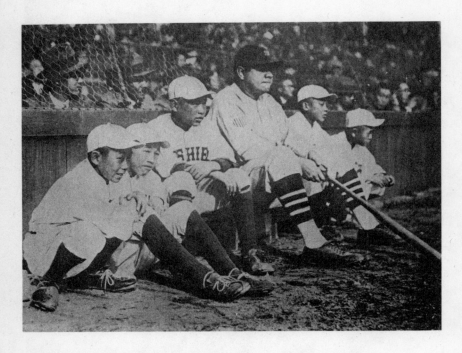

Doing what he loved best—Japan, 1936.

With blind children in Yokohama. (photo courtesy National Baseball Library, Cooperstown, NY)

The cover of a Japanese sports magazine.

SF1699-3/7-KOBE,JAPAN: A memorial in honor of the late Babe Ruth is unveiled at Koshein Stadium here (2/26). Capt. Edward C. Broadhurst (center,with his wife,Louise),of Ravenna, Ohio, gave the chief address. U.S.Signal Corps photo via ACME TELEPHOTO

The unveiling of a memorial to my father at Koshein Stadium in Kobe, Japan. Captain Edward C. Broadhurst (shown here with his wife Louise) of Ravenna, Ohio, gave the chief address. (photo courtesy National Baseball Library, Cooperstown, NY)

My husband Dominick and I in Nevada in 1948.

Dominick and I at Babe Ruth Day at Yankee Stadium—that's Juanita sitting behind us at Dominick's shoulder.

Some of the members of the Red Sox' all-time "Dream Team" at a Boston Baseball Writers dinner, which was held at the Sheraton Boston Hotel on January 27, 1983. I am standing with Rick Burleson; behind us (from left to right) are Carlton Fisk, Dwight Evans, Carl Yastrzemski, Bobby Doerr, Rico Petrocelli and Dick Radatz. (photo by Mike Anderson)

At my father's stamp cancellation ceremony in Baltimore, Maryland, in 1983. My hand is being held by U.S. Postmaster Warren M. Bloomberg. Behind us (from left to right) are John J. Foster, Jr., Dominick, our daughter Linda, and Paul Welsh.

Dad at the Polo Grounds in August 1922.

12

Making Up Ground

When I was still living at home, Joseph Kelly, one of the heirs to the Gillette Razor fortune, called one night from France to ask me if I would join him in Paris and get married. He was a relative of a girlfriend of mine and a bit brazen for a twenty-one year old. I was only sixteen and had dated him a couple of times, but certainly not enough to take his marriage proposal seriously, so I declined his offer.

Little did I know that Dad had been listening in on our entire conversation on the telephone in his bedroom. As soon as Joseph hung up, he came storming into my room, yelling at the top of his lungs, "Who the hell was that guy? What's going on around here? You're not old enough to know when your diapers are dry!" I had never seen my father so crazed. I couldn't imagine what he would have done if my answer had been "yes."

The next time I got a proposal, I decided to marry. I had been living with my girlfriend Pamela for nearly two years, supporting myself on the interest from the money Helen had left to me, when I met a relative of Pamela's named

Daniel. After six months we were married, on January 7, 1940, in a very simple ceremony—just a minister, a best man and a maid of honor were present. I didn't invite my father to the ceremony because I was sure he disapproved. When I eventually got up enough nerve to call him, he didn't have much of a reaction; he was simply disappointed and thought I had made a big mistake. "It's your bed and your the one who has to lie in it" was all he said. In October I had my first child, Daniel Junior.

As it turned out, Dad was right. I realize now that I probably married my first husband more out of need for companionship and security than genuine love. The ill-fated marriage lasted only five years, but during that time I bore three children and learned a great deal about myself and the world around me.

When Danny was born, I felt like I was finally on my way to finding my own identity. I was on top of the world. Danny was mine, and nobody could take him away from me. I was only twenty at the time, and probably not ready for children, but somehow that thought never crossed my mind. I looked forward to having another child as soon as possible, because I didn't want Danny to be an only child; after all, I knew what it was like to grow up with no one to relate to or share your emotions with. I vowed that I would never do to my children what had been done to me. I would be fair, I would love them, and I would never leave them, no matter what happened down the road.

Within four years, Danny had two sisters, Genevieve and Ellen, and I had my hands full. Shortly after Ellen was born, my husband and I decided that our relationship was not making either of us happy. There was no time to feel sorry for myself; after our divorce, I retained custody of the children and our house on Long Island. I readied myself for life as a single parent.

It had taken me a long time to realize that I was my own person, and that there was a place for everybody in this world, it was just a matter of finding your niche. Adversity doesn't always bring out the best in people, but in my case it did. Instead of having someone point out my mistakes all the time, I learned from them on my own. We had our share of bumps and bruises along the way, but I feel I did a good job of holding the family together.

Under normal circumstances, the financial burdens would have been enormous, but I still had the money that Helen had left to me, which was more than enough to live on. From time to time Babe offered me money, but I never accepted a penny. I was determined to make it on my own, so I always said that everything was just fine.

Initially, my marriage caused some strife between my father and me. Since Babe had been against it from the start, I wasn't surprised, but as time passed the friction seemed to subside. Neither of us made an issue out of what had happened; instead we tried to forget the past and concentrate on improving our relationship.

Dad took great pride in his grandchildren, so it was a shame that he was unable to spend more time with them. When Danny was about two years old, he had this terrible rash on his behind. My father, trying to help, pulled down his pants and put zinc oxide all over it. It didn't work, but I never told Babe that—he thought zinc oxide cured everything.

After a while I began to consider remarriage, but unfortunately most of the men I dated were overwhelmed when I told them that I already had three children. Yet one night, a girlfriend invited me to her apartment and introduced me to Dominick Pirone. My first words to him were "My three children and I are very pleased to meet you." He smiled and didn't seem the least bit fazed. "Oh, that's nice" was all he said.

We had a lengthy conversation that evening and he eventually drove me home. Dominick was intelligent, handsome and very gentle, and I sensed that he had a warm heart. We dated regularly for a few months and then got married.

We moved to Dyre Avenue in the Bronx and had three children of our own by 1954: Donna, Richard and Linda. For the first time in my life, I didn't feel that I was constantly looking over my shoulder. Six children didn't allow for much free time, as you can imagine, but I had no complaints. The children were well behaved and stayed out of trouble—for the most part. I do remember one instance when Danny and Gene were caught stealing pretzels from a nearby bar. They told the owner that they were hungry because they never had anything to eat at home. Believe me, it was quite a shock when the Children's Aid Society knocked at my door. Some behinds were red that night.

The children helped heal some of the old wounds, and my father and I were able to talk to each other more easily without Claire's interference. One of our favorite meeting places was the barbershop at the Ansonia Hotel on the West side of Manhattan. Dad used to go there every morning for a shave and a manicure and, when necessary, a haircut. He loved it when I brought along the children; he would make funny faces for them and bounce them up and down on his knee.

When I could manage a day away from my family, I would meet Babe at the golf course to keep him company while he played eighteen holes. I really didn't care much for the game, but it was an opportunity to spend time together, as well as a relaxing way to spend an afternoon. Dad thoroughly enjoyed golfing and in all likelihood could have turned professional had he so desired, but he told me that he never wanted to play professionally, he only wanted to play for fun. He consistently shot in the low seventies and occasionally demonstrated that familiar Ruthian power stroke off the tee with 300-yard drives.

Once he played a tournament in Suffern, New York, with Babe Didrikson, the celebrated female athlete. After the tournament that evening they drove back to New York City together in his car. On a rain-slicked highway the car overturned; luckily both Babes were unhurt. That was by no means my father's first accident. He had a history of automobile wrecks and miraculously managed to walk away from every one. However, one Philadelphia newspaper did erroneously proclaim his death after one such incident.

Dad was impulsive when it came to buying cars and would not hesitate a second if he saw one he liked. He once paid cash for a brand-new car, had the Boston car dealer fill the gas tank, and then drove it right off the showroom floor. On his way to New York, he lost control of the car in Tracy, Connecticut, hitting a bridge abutment and ending up in a ditch. As two farmers approached the car, hoping to find the driver alive, my father climbed out of the window of the overturned vehicle, dusted himself off and waved hello. He was a bit rattled but, as usual, unscathed. Incredibly, a policeman drove him to Meriden, Connecticut, where he bought another new Packard from Scanlon Packard. He paid in cash, requested another full tank and drove to New York.

My father remained in demand after his retirement in 1935. He picked annual all-star teams, went to the World Series, traveled around the world, and played in exhibition games. I accompanied him out west for one of those exhibition tours, for which he was paid the handsome sum of $20,000—all in silver dollars! I'll never forget the time I had, trying to carry all of those sacks of silver into a Denver bank.

On June 12, 1939, Babe gave a moving speech at the formal opening at the Baseball Hall of Fame in Cooperstown, New York. The opening of the Hall of Fame was not only a banner day for all of major league baseball, it was also twenty-five years, minus one day, after he had pitched his first game for the Boston Red Sox. Babe had been inducted three years earlier; other players, such as Tris Speaker, Cy Young and Grover Cleveland Alexander, were elected by the baseball writers over the next few years. But it wasn't until 1939, the one-hundredth anniversary of baseball, that the official dedication took place.

My father symbolically pointed at two little boys sitting in front of the lectern as he began his speech. "They started something," he boomed, "and the kids are keeping the ball rolling. I hope some of you kids will be in the Hall of Fame. And I hope the youngsters of today have the same opportunity to experience such a feeling."

In the early 1940s Dad continued going strong. His voice was heard on weekly radio broadcasts, and he played himself in *Pride of the Yankees,* a 1941 movie about his dear friend, Lou Gehrig. But in 1945 his hectic schedule began to take its toll on his health. Suffering from exhaustion and a nervous breakdown, he was admitted to the Fitch Sanitarium in the Bronx.

When I visited him in the hospital, he asked me to bring him back some blank checks from his checkbook so he could buy cigars, newspapers and other sundries. There was only one minor problem: In order to get the checks, I had to sneak back into the apartment, where I was not welcome. I was petrified at the thought of Claire catching me, but luckily for me, no one was home.

While he was in the hospital, Babe repeatedly complained about Claire. "I can't stand her, and I don't want to go back to her," he told me. He desperately pleaded with me to find him a place in the country. He had always loved the outdoors, but Claire had "this thing" for New York, like it was the only city in the world. Anytime Dad suggested moving, Claire refused.

I don't know why he never divorced Claire. When she pressured him about Helen back in the twenties, he always said that he could not get a divorce since he was a Catholic. It's possible that he believed in the sacrament of marriage so strongly that he simply would not entertain the thought, but I can't say for sure if that was the only reason.

After three weeks in the hospital, Babe was released, and, true to form, he went right back to Claire. He had won a tough physical battle during his stay in the hospital, but the cancer that was soon to take his life was rapidly spreading, undiscovered. My father would soon be fighting for his life, not just his sanity.

By 1948 Dominick and I had relocated with the family to Connecticut, but we frequently made the trip to Long Island for Sunday dinner with Charlie and Juanita. Over the years they had become like parents to me, and the kids treated them as though they were part of the family, referring to them as "Uncle Charlie" and "Aunt Nita."

During the next fifteen years life was much less complicated. After having suffered through such a traumatic childhood, adolescence and early adult life, I was truly relieved to finally be part of a stable environment. I tried my best to give all my children as much care and attention as possible, because I wanted them to understand the true meaning of the word love.

Ruth's Rival Denies Love
As U. S. Hunts Dope Trail

A recent photo of Dorothy Ruth, now in Academy of Assumption at Wellesley.

Babe Ruth, the husband of the dead woman and hero of baseball diamond.

This NEWS photo of the late Mrs. Ruth brought about her identification when it was shown to neighbors.

Dr. E. H. Kinder, with whom Mrs. Ruth lived, who surrendered yesterday.

Mrs. Gertrude Nason, a neighbor of Mrs. Ruth, who helped identify the body.

Gloria Bishop's Divorce Waiting Arrival in Reno

(Special to the DAILY NEWS)

Gloria Gould Bishop

Reno, Nev., Jan. 14.—Gloria Gould Bishop is expected to arrive here tonight for final action in the divorce suit she filed last August against Henry A. Bishop jr., scion of one of Connecticut's proudest families.

Speculation is rife concerning what will be done with Gloria's daughter, Gloria, in the event that Gloria gets her decree—which she asked for on grounds, it was said, of extreme cruelty.

Gloria, dancing daughter of George Jay Gould, mixes a frank love of the joys of Broadway with a deep attachment for her child.

When the baby came, a little more than three years ago, she told of her bliss thus:

"I am through with society. All that is froth. No woman enjoys life to the full until she has known the joys of motherhood. The name Gloia is Italian for joy.

But, apparently, the marital troubles that have haunted more than one Gould did not, pass by George Jay's daughter. In 1923 she established residence in Paris—for a divorce, it was said. But she rejoined Henry. In 1927 she again went to Paris, but no open break developed.

Before she betook herself to Reno, she remarked: "If ever my home is wrecked, it will be because of my love for my baby."

Gloria became the bride of Bishop when she was 17, in a simple ceremony at St. Bartholomew's church on Park ave. Bishop is the son of Henry Alfred Bishop.

Marshal Foch Slightly Better

Paris, Jan. 14 (I.N.S.)—A very slight improvement was noted late this afternoon in the condition of Marshal Ferdinand Foch, famous war-time generalissimo, who is critically ill at his home here of heart disease. The marshal was extremely low, however, and his death was expected at any time.

Gilda Gets Her Divorce As Quick as a Shake

"He tore four gowns and an ermine coat off me," that was what Gilda Gray, pictured here, told the judge yesterday. And did she win that divorce? She did.

Gilda declared that Gil used to beat her up so that she had to use grease paint to hide the scars before she went out to dance her nightly shimmy.

When the decree sad been handed

(Continued on page 11)

Gil Gets About $200,000 By Way of Settlement.

(Special to the DAILY NEWS)

Waukesha, Wis., Jan. 14.—"And so they were divorced, and lived happily ever after."

Being the caption for the final fadeout in that film (with sound), "Up While the City Sleeps," or "The Night Club Love Life of Gilda Gray and her Boogie Man, Gil Boag."

Gilda Gray, hot mamma of the shimmy, took the stand in Circuit court here today and gave Gil such a verbal slamming that Judge C. M. Tabison handed her the decision of the spot. Being recounted in New York, and thus, in the eyes of the court, took everything on the spot without lifting as much as an eyebrow of remonstrance.

Doctor Stole Heart As Well As Tonsils, etc., Says Model

By Irene Kuhn

Her broken heart is worth considerably more to Miss Edna Fields, 21-year-old dress model, than her tonsils, appendix and other portions of her anatomy which she lost via the operation route to Dr. Max B. Rice, former society surgeon now in prison, convicted of murder, and the

(Continued on page 21)

Dentist Cleared in Death; Babe Faces Kin's Hate

By FRANK DOLAN

BOSTON, Jan. 15.—The embers of the fire fatal to Mrs. Helen Ruth, wife of the Babe, last Friday night, sent their glare on the two men most prominent in her life, the ball player and Dr. Edward H. Kinder, and drew Federal narcotic agents into the investigation today.

Dr. Kinder, dentist, in whose Watertown home she lived as Mrs. Ruth—a home paid for in part, police say, with proceeds of the Babe's home runs—scurried into police headquarters today.

The dentist, missing since the fire, had been in hiding at the home of his parents, Mr. and Mrs. William F. Kinder.

Asked About Opium.

Dr. Kinder's father, who lives at 606 East 7th st., South Boston, denied this evening reports he had threatened Ruth with exposure if he accused his son wrongly.

"Ruth is a hell of a good fellow; I know him well," said the elder Kinder.

Asked about reports from New York that Mrs. Ruth had said she knew a Boston doctor who could furnish her with opium, William Kinder said:

"I'm not in a position to talk about that now."

While state authorities appeared to be satisfied Mrs. Ruth met her death by accident, federal narcotic agents were understood tonight to be investigating Dr. Kinder's activities to see if drugs may have figured in the death.

Denies Calling Her Wife.

After his two-hour conference with Chief John Millmore of Watertown Dr. Kinder scurried out to issue a statement through his lawyer, James F. Vahey, denying that he had lived with Mrs. Ruth as man and wife.

"Kinder never said," Vahey told reporters, "that he was married to Mrs. Ruth. She was nothing to him but a good friend."

This statement collided head-on with the discovery by police of canceled checks in the modest Kinder home. The checks, indicating that Mrs. Ruth had been on the Bambino's payroll for about $10,000 a year, showed that she had spent money to maintain herself and Kinder.

Bought House and Auto.

Watertown police and neighbors regarded it as significant that just after Mrs. Ruth appeared in Watertown as Kinder's constant companion he bought the house she died in, assessed at $4,500, and a Packard sedan.

The broken-hearted Babe tonight issued his second statement since the tragedy. He said:

"There is plenty to talk about in

(Continued on page 4, col. 1)

Ice—115 Years Ago

On June 11, 1814, the following advertisement appeared in the Alexandria (Va.) Gazette:

"Those who wish to become subscribers for ice for the season are informed that it is now ready to be delivered to them daily. Terms, six pounds per day, as long as the ice may last, for six dollars; the season ending on the 10th day of September."

Today there is no "season" for ice and no danger of a shortage.

Knickerbocker
ICE
Company

13

Intentionally Passed

At one point in Babe's illustrious career he said that he would be satisfied if he hit seven hundred home runs, appeared in ten World Series, played twenty seasons, and managed in the big leagues. He hit his seven hundredth home run on July 13, 1934, appeared in his tenth World Series in 1932, and played in his twentieth season in 1933; yet he never fulfilled his greatest dream: to manage a major league team. He died bitterly disappointed that the call for which he had waited his entire life never came.

On September 25, 1929, the New York Yankees were dealt a tragic blow when their long-time manager and friend, Miller Huggins, died. The legendary Huggins, winner of six pennants and three World Series from 1921 to 1928, would be sorely missed, and finding a capable replacement would be a chore. As the season ended, many names were tossed around as potential successors—one of them Babe's.

Besides being a proficient home-run hitter in 1929, my father believed that he was legitimate managerial timber as well; unfortunately, the Yankees did not share his beliefs and never took him seriously. Colonel Jacob Ruppert convinced Babe that he had at least two or three good playing years left, and that the Yankees would benefit most from his services on the field, not in the dugout. What Ruppert did not realize was that Babe had no intentions of quitting; he wanted to be a player/manager like his famous contemporaries Ty Cobb, Rogers Hornsby and Tris Speaker.

However, after numerous discussions with Jacob Ruppert and Ed Barrow, Babe allowed himself to be convinced and took himself out of the running. "Colonel Ruppert and I," he declared, "agree that it would be unwise for me to become manager now. I still have two or three good years left. Someday I hope to be a manager, but I'm willing to wait."

Ex-Yankee Bob Shawkey, a 37-year-old right-handed pitcher, was hired to replace Huggins. Shawkey, a solid baseball man, had been a coach with the Yankees in 1929, but he had no prior managerial experience. Following in the footsteps of the diminutive Huggins proved to be no easy task, and a lack of discipline and breakdown in communication with many of his former teammates led to Shawkey's undoing. The Yankees finished a disappointing third that year, and, never satisfied with mediocrity, the Yankee brass immediately began its search for a new helmsman.

Once again, Babe reasoned that he was the logical choice and took his case to Colonel Ruppert. "Colonel, if you're serious about finding a new manager, I want the job," he implored. "I think I've earned the chance."

Ruppert frowned. This was not just another whim. Dad was dead serious, and so Ruppert knew he would have to be truthful. "Look, Babe," the Colonel said. "You didn't take care of yourself for many years. Can I turn my team over to a man who often doesn't take the right things seriously?"

Babe was hurt. "All right, Colonel," he said somberly. "You're the boss."

The search for a new manager did not take Ruppert and Barrow very long. Quickly a meeting was set up with Joe

McCarthy, the recently dismissed manager of the Chicago Cubs. McCarthy had won the pennant in 1929 but was axed in 1930 after his club fell to second place.

The day after the 1930 World Series, it was announced to the New York media that McCarthy and the Yankees had agreed to terms. Everyone in New York applauded his hiring—except Babe. He was furious because he felt he should have been chosen instead.

From the beginning Babe resented McCarthy, and most of the Yankees knew it, especially Joe. McCarthy was an authoritative, no-nonsense disciplinarian who demanded respect and sound fundamental baseball from all of his players. Somehow he never let the hostility that existed between himself and my father interfere with the operation and performance of his ballclub.

Despite Babe's antagonistic behavior, McCarthy judiciously avoided any direct confrontation with my father, and by 1932 the Yankees were once again on top of the baseball world, with Babe contributing in a big way.

After the victory over the Cubs in the 1932 World Series, Joe McCarthy was rewarded with a three-year extension of his contract, a devastating blow to Babe's hopes. It seemed clear that the Yankees had slammed the door in his face and forced him to look for an opening with one of the other major league clubs.

One of the first nibbles came from the Boston Red Sox. Tom Yawkey had purchased the club in 1933 and believed that the return of Babe to Boston, the team with which he began his career, was a natural. Babe's heroics as a left-handed pitcher had propelled the Red Sox to three World Series championships in four years, 1915-1918, a height which they failed to reach after his departure. Many Red Sox supporters were still very bitter about losing Babe in 1920, when owner Harry Frazee had sold him to the New York Yankees, and he was still immensely popular in Boston. Yawkey believed that signing Babe would benefit not only the Red Sox but the entire city, but general manager Eddie Collins did not share Yawkey's enthusiasm and convinced him that Babe was not the answer. In October of the following year Yawkey bought Joe Cronin from the Washington Senators and signed him to a five-year contract as player/manager.

After the 1933 season the Detroit Tigers also expressed an interest in Babe; Frank Navin, the owner of the Tigers, was willing to take a chance, and a tentative agreement was worked out with the Yankees. All that remained was for Babe to meet with Navin in person and iron out the details. There was only one obstacle—Claire. Her exact quote was "Who are you to go to them? Let them come to you!"

Dad had arranged to play a series of exhibition games in Honolulu, and he figured that he could meet with Navin when he returned. Ed Barrow suggested that Babe delay his trip to Hawaii for one day, stop in Detroit on his way to San Francisco, and settle things once and for all. Babe disagreed. "You're making a mistake," Barrow told him. "You better go see him now."

Babe responded, "There's plenty of time. The season doesn't begin for six months. I've got things all set in Hawaii. I'll call him when I get back." Dad left Navin hanging and departed for San Francisco.

Once he arrived, however, he obviously changed his mind and made a spontaneous telephone call to Navin in the middle of the night. "This is Babe Ruth. I'm calling from San Francisco to find out if you want me as manager. I'm leaving for Hawaii and I want an answer right now—yes or no!"

Navin, irritated at being awakened at two o'clock in the morning, fired back, "Since you put it that way, the answer is no!" Shortly afterward, Navin bought Mickey Cochrane from Connie Mack and named him manager of the Tigers.

By 1934 it was becoming increasingly obvious that my father's days with the Yankees were numbered, but because of his popularity with the fans, the situation had to be handled delicately. The Yankees couldn't just toss him aside like a tattered baseball; they hoped he would leave with dignity—on his own.

Barrow decided to acquiesce to Babe's demands and give him an opportunity to demonstrate his ability as a manager, but on the minor-league level. Dad was offered the job of managing the Yankee's farm club in Newark, New Jersey, in the International League, but he considered the proposition a demotion and promptly rejected it. "I'm a big-leaguer," he said. "Why should I have to go to the minors first? Cobb and Speaker didn't. Why do I have to?"

After Babe cooled down, he went home to talk it over with Claire. She told him under no circumstances should he accept the job, that it would be a disgrace for the great Babe Ruth to go to the bush leagues. She was able to convince him that many big-league jobs would be opening up in the near future, and then he would have his pick.

By 1934 Babe's legs had slowed as much as his bat. He hit a disappointing .288, his lowest average in eighteen years, with only twenty-two homers. In addition, it was beginning to dawn on him that the Yankees were no longer interested in his playing services. This might be his last chance to wrestle the managerial reins away from Joe McCarthy, he figured, and before he left for the World Series Dad put the question to Jacob Ruppert for the last time. "Are you satisfied with McCarthy as your manager?" he asked candidly.

"Why, yes," Ruppert answered. "Of course I am. Aren't you?"

"No, I'm not. I know I can do a better job than he can."

"Really? Well, that's too bad, Ruth. I'm sorry, but McCarthy is the manager and he will continue as manager."

"That suits me," Babe said proudly. "That's all I wanted to know." He made up his mind that if he couldn't manage the Yankees, he wasn't going to play for them, either.

At the World Series, a number of writers confronted him about his current status. "I'm through with the Yankees," Babe bellowed. "I won't play with them again unless I can manage. They're sticking with McCarthy, and that lets me out."

After the World Series, Babe set sail for the Orient on his most exotic barnstorming trip to date. The Americans played to sell-out crowds everywhere, including Tokyo, Osaka, Shanghai and Manila.

Meanwhile, back in New York, Babe's future remained hot copy for the sports pages. In an article from the *New York Times* dated November 1, 1934, an owner who wished to remain anonymous commented on the prospects of Babe becoming a manager. "Ruth unquestionably has the background, the personality and many of the qualifications essential to becoming a successful manager," the owner remarked. "There should be a spot where he could have a chance to show what he could do with a ballclub, but frankly I don't know anybody willing to undertake the experiment. The big question concerns Ruth's ability to maintain discipline. He has never had such responsibility."

While Babe was on the barnstorming trip, Connie Mack of the Philadelphia Athletics was contemplating retirement. He wanted to turn the club over to Dad, but he changed his mind when he realized that Babe wasn't the only risk. "I couldn't have made Babe a manager," Mack said later. "His wife would have been running the club in a month."

During this time, negotiations were taking place between Colonel Ruppert and Judge Emil Fuchs, owner of the Boston Braves. Babe returned to New York on February 20, 1935, and within a week he was no longer a Yankee. On February 26, 1935, his glorious career with the New York Yankees came to an end when they gave him his unconditional release.

Waiting in the wings was Judge Fuchs, who promised my father everything but ownership of the Braves to induce him into signing a contract. Besides making him vice president and assistant manager, Fuchs promised Babe that he would take over for Bill McKechnie, the Braves' current manager, as soon as McKechnie's contract expired at the end of the season. Babe never made it to the end of the season. In less than two months, on June 2, 1935, Babe quit baseball, thoroughly disgusted with Fuchs. The judge not only used Babe to hype ticket sales, he also persuaded him to appear at the opening of one of his *stores*. Dad realized that Fuchs was looking for a circus attraction, not a manager.

Once Babe quit, he joined the ranks of the unemployed. He decided to relax and spend more time with his family. Deep down he felt that he belonged in baseball, the game to which he had devoted his entire life, and before long, he was sure, he would be fielding offers from major league clubs. He was shocked, therefore, when over the three-year period of 1935-37 only three new managers were hired. During the last few years of his career, his timing was way off.

Babe remained out of baseball's select fraternity for more than three years, until Larry MacPhail, the new executive vice president of the Brooklyn Dodgers, signed him as a first-base coach and hitting instructor. The Dodgers finished in the second division in 1938, but my father still felt the season was a rousing success. He was back in baseball and the prospects of managing the Brooklyn club looked promising. But Larry MacPhail had made other plans.

MacPhail was looking at Leo Durocher, the Dodgers' fiesty shortstop, not Babe, as Burleigh Grimes's successor. Leo was the logical, if not the sentimental, choice to replace Grimes, because for most of the campaign he had served as team captain and Burleigh's right-hand man.

The interesting aspect about the hiring of Leo Durocher was that Larry MacPhail didn't get along with him; in the book *The Roaring Redhead*, Don Warfield and Lee Mac-Phail write, "Larry didn't want Durocher and pointed out at least five reasons for turning him down, including Durocher's inability to handle his own affairs." MacPhail and Durocher must have reconciled their differences rather quickly, because during the World Series he broke the news to Leo that he would be Brooklyn's new manager in 1939.

Durocher and my father had an ongoing feud dating back to the late 1920s, when Leo was a reserve shortstop for the Yankees, and their mutual distaste for one another never subsided. Durocher and Grimes's behind-the-back remarks and public criticism regarding Babe's coaching ability did nothing to further his cause, and once Durocher was officially hired on October 13, Babe hung up his spikes, this time for good. Although only in his early forties, he was a forgotten man, relegated to listening to games on the radio. At home, he often managed from his armchair, calling the plays and making the substitutions before they happened. There should have been a job for him somewhere in baseball, but baseball's attitude was, Out of sight, out of mind.

During Babe's career, more than twenty of his peers managed in the major leagues without prior experience, including Walter Johnson, Mickey Cochrane and Bill Terry. Was there a conscious effort to keep Babe out of baseball? Maybe. One theory of the day suggested that Babe had been "blacklisted" by some of the owners for changing the salary structure of major league baseball. The truth was that players *did* use Babe's salary as a yardstick during their own negotiations. For example, one above-average player reasoned that "if Babe was worth $80,000 a year, I must be worth at least half or a third of that."

Babe tried to enjoy retirement by hunting, fishing and playing golf, but in the back of his mind he kept wondering why the owners had collectively deserted him. "What do I have to do to become a manager?" he often asked. "They tried me out for twenty-two years and ought to know what I've got.

"Do I think I'd make a good manager? Sure I do! I know as much baseball as anyone today, and I don't forget what I know. Pitchers gave me more than two thousand passes. But I can't get to first base with the magnates."

Two years later, on July 28, 1943, Babe finally got a chance to manage a team of big-leaguers at Yankee Stadium—a charity game for the Red Cross and the War Relief Fund.

The ownership of the Yankees changed hands in 1945, with Larry MacPhail, Dan Topping and Del Webb assuming control of the club. With MacPhail in charge, Babe felt he had his best opportunity to get back into baseball. He was no longer demanding anything; he was begging. It was not the first time my father had pleaded with Yankee management for a job; in 1935 he had offered to manage the club for one dollar—but was turned down!

After several letters to MacPhail went unanswered, Babe finally telephoned. The conversation was upbeat and optimistic, with MacPhail definitely expressing interest in Babe's services. The call ended on Larry's "Sit tight, Babe. You'll hear from us." He never heard a word.

Even more frustrating was the year 1946, as the Yankees changed managers three times without ever giving Dad the slightest consideration. Joe McCarthy, winner of eight pennants and seven World Series in fifteen years with the Yankees, resigned in May because of differences with Mac-Phail, as well as reported stomach problems. All-Star catcher Bill Dickey, in the twilight of a brilliant career with the Yankees, replaced McCarthy, but the team continued to lose and Dickey was dismissed in early September, with New York well out of the pennant race. Finally, Johnny Neun, a former first baseman with the Detroit Tigers and the Boston Braves, was hired as interim manager, temporarily filling the void until the Yankees chose Bucky Harris as their pilot for 1947.

On September 20, 1946, shortly before the end of the season, Babe made his final attempt in a letter to Larry Mac-Phail requesting any job in the Yankees organization. This time at least he got an answer.

On October 20, a letter arrived from the Yankees. "That's bad news," said Babe. "When it's good news they telephone." Dad was right. MacPhail did not want him, and told him so in what amounted to a polite brush off. In the letter, Mac-Phail explained why hiring Bill Dickey the previous year had been a mistake, one that he did not intend to repeat. "When Mr. McCarthy resigned during the season, it was practically everyone's opinion that Dickey was entitled to a chance with the club. Lack of experience handicapped Bill in meeting present problems and would, I am convinced, similarly handicap anyone else who had not managed elsewhere." MacPhail also suggested that Babe should forget about major league baseball and concentrate his efforts on the amateur level. "There is an important job to be done in the Metropolitan New York area in connection with the promotion of sandlot and amateur baseball," wrote MacPhail.

After reading the letter, Dad put his head in his hands and cried. I hurt so much for him, but I was powerless to help him. All I could say was "I'm sorry." He just stood up and slowly walked into his bedroom and shut the door. I felt that baseball had used him for all those years, after all he had given to the game. He had accumulated so much knowledge that he would not be allowed to put into use. To this day, I feel that baseball made a big mistake.

Dad had been slapped in the face for what he thought was the last time, but the worst was yet to come. In November of 1946 his despondency reached an all-time low. His marriage to Claire had been steadily eroding, returning to baseball seemed remote at best, and, perhaps worst of all, he began to experience excruciatingly painful headaches. No one knew it at the time, but the discomfort he was feeling was caused by a malignant growth in the left side of his neck that had yet to be diagnosed.

A few weeks later, at about eleven o'clock in the evening, I received a frantic phone call from a friend telling me to rush over to Babe and Claire's apartment on Riverside Drive. When I arrived, his bedroom door was locked, and I could hear my emotionally distraught father threatening to jump from the fifteenth-floor window. I got on my knees and looked through the keyhole, only to discover Babe trying to break the window guard by jumping up and down on the chain. I felt completely helpless, trying to console him from out in the hallway; I just wanted to throw my arms around him and tell him how much he meant to me. I don't remember what I said, but thank God he finally came to his senses and opened the door.

If you were wondering where Claire was while all this was going on, she was in the next room—*reading*.

14

No More Encores

On August 16, 1948, at 7:31
P.M., my father closed his eyes and went into a coma. At
8:01 P.M. he was pronounced dead. That final half hour of
his life was the first time in almost two years that he had
had any real peace and quiet, both mentally and physically. My father had fought hard but finally lost the battle with
cancer that had begun two years earlier.

In November of 1946 Babe reluctantly checked into
French Hospital in New York City for routine tests after complaining of severe headache pain for more than two months.
The test results were worse than anyone expected—Babe
was suffering from cancer.

As the rest of the world speculated as to the seriousness
of my father's illness, I knew. A family doctor had come
to my house to treat a friend for a minor illness, and I
overheard him telling his patient that he had attended an
American Medical Association meeting where Dad's condition was discussed. The doctors had found an inoperable
tumor at the base of his brain, and the prognosis was that
Babe Ruth had two years at the most to live. When the doc-

tor realized that I had overheard him, he begged me to keep it a secret.

Comprehension was a long time in coming. I couldn't believe how something so horrible could be happening to our family—and it was brutal knowing that my father was dying yet not being able to tell him or anyone else about it.

After months of agony, an emergency operation was performed in the spring of 1947, with the hopes of removing the growth from the left side of his neck. Tragically, the cancer had spread to the point where it could not be completely removed, and, worst of all, the remaining tumor continued to grow. As the pain increased, so did the doses of morphine. The sensitive nature of the tumor prevented him from sleeping or eating solid foods. My father was slowly wasting away.

Sunday, April 27, 1947, was proclaimed Babe Ruth Day in the major leagues by A. B. "Happy" Chandler, the new commissioner of baseball, and as part of the nationwide ceremonies, Babe's speech from Yankee Stadium would be broadcast live to all other ballparks. At a time when most of baseball had forgotten about my father, Happy Chandler reunited him with the game.

People had read about my father's three-month stay in French Hospital, but since then he had been out of the public eye, recuperating in Florida and California. When he appeared at Yankee Stadium that day, the seriousness of his illness was now in full view. His once hulking frame had been reduced to skin and bones, and his normally resonant voice was nothing more than a croaking whisper. When it was finally my father's turn at the microphone, all of major league baseball was listening.

He wasn't bitter, only disappointed at the way baseball had treated him since he left the game. For that reason, he did not thank baseball or the Yankees but directed his remarks toward the youth of America. They were always the ones who mattered most.

"You know," he began, "this baseball game of ours comes up from the youth. That means the boys. After you've been a boy who's grown up learning how to play ball, then you come to the boys you see representing themselves today in our national pastime. The only real game in the world, I think, is baseball. As a rule, some people think if you give them a football or something like that, naturally, they're athletes right away. You can't do that in baseball. You've got to start way down, at the bottom, when you're six or seven years old. You can't wait until you're fifteen or sixteen. You've got to let it grow up with you, and if you're successful and try hard enough, you're bound to come out on top.

"There's been so many lovely things said about me. I'm glad I had an opportunity to thank everybody. Thank you." Babe acknowledged the cheers of the capacity crowd, then disappeared into the Yankee dugout.

His health worsened by June of 1947, and as a last resort, he underwent treatment with teropterin, an experimental drug which had shown promise in checking cancer in mice. His treatments began on June 29, 1947, and within six weeks his condition improved dramatically. A thorough examination on August 14 produced the following results: "The mass in the neck disappeared completely. His pain has practically gone. He eats solid food without any difficulty in swallowing. The voice has improved a great deal. He has gained twelve pounds in weight." The doctor's report added, however, "We are naturally aware that the excellent results in this one case may only be temporary."

The remission of the cancer was short-lived, leaving my father confused and painfully ill. Despite this fact, during the next six months he continued to make public appearances and worked for the Ford Motor Company promoting American Legion baseball. But on January 10, 1948, his failing health necessitated his return to the hospital for three more operations.

One of my father's last public appearances was at Yankee Stadium's Silver Jubilee celebration on June 13, 1948. Twenty-five years earlier, Babe had appropriately christened the stadium with its first home run, and part of the ceremonies included the retiring of his famed number 3.

After his former teammates had been introduced, all eyes turned to the top step of the dugout. In one of the most familiar sights in the history of Yankee Stadium, Babe Ruth left the dugout and headed for home plate with a bat clutched in his left hand, only this time he wasn't going to swing for the fences. Because of his weak physical condition, he needed the bat to hold himself up.

With tears running down his face, he spoke to the fans for a final time. "Ladies and gentlemen," he began. "I just want to say one thing. I am proud I hit the first home run here in 1923. It was marvelous to see thirteen or fourteen players who were my teammates going back twenty-five years. I'm telling you it makes me proud and happy to be here. Thank you."

He acknowledged the cheers of the crowd as he slowly made his way toward the dugout. It was clear that Babe had taken his final bow. There would be no more encores.

My father checked into Memorial Hospital in Manhattan on June 24, knowing full well that he was dying; the hospital treated mostly cancer patients. Ironically, he had spent many moments of his life entertaining children in that very hospital, trying to raise their spirits.

The sportswriters of the day had made a pact never to print a word about Babe's illness. Although many people have stated that Babe did not know that he had cancer until the last few weeks of his life, when he checked into Memorial Hospital he was well aware of his illness. It wasn't a topic that he discussed with the writers, nor they with him. Knowing that he was an avid reader of the sports pages, most likely they were afraid of revealing the extent of his illness to him. I thank them for their respect, because they really could have had a field day with the story.

My father's last public appearance was at the Astor Theatre for the premiere of the film depiction of his life, *The Babe Ruth Story*, on July 26, 1948. It was also Babe Ruth Day in New York City. When they were making the film, starring William Bendix as Babe, my father had gone to Hollywood as a technical advisor. The producers had promised that he would have the final say regarding the content of the film.

The night he left the hospital to attend the premiere, he had to be carried out the front door; his "good" friends were responsible for dragging him out of his hospital bed. When he got out of the car in front of the theater, he had no idea where he was because of the amount of drugs that were in his system. It was one of the cruelest scenes that I have ever witnessed in my life.

I was totally taken by surprise. When I had left Dad that afternoon he was sedated, and I had no idea that he would be at the theater that evening. Intentionally my permisson had not been asked, because the people who took him to the premiere knew that there was no way I would have allowed it. As I later found out, the nurses and doctors were also kept in the dark. It occurred to me that there was only one person who could have bypassed the security guards so easily—Claire. When I confronted her, she admitted that she was responsible. She told me that it was necessary for him to be there and, after all, no harm had been done. Once again, her heartless, selfish motives caused Dad unnecessary grief, and in this case, turned the evening into a circus sideshow. No harm, indeed!

Babe was at the mercy of a wild and frenzied crowd, which pushed and waved paper for autographs in his face. There was no expression in his eyes. He was just a zombie. I stood by helplessly; if only there was something I could do to stop the nightmare. Finally, I was so disgusted that I gave my ticket to someone else and went home. After a short time, my father was allowed to leave a film which he never realized he was watching and was returned to the hospital.

That night left such a bad taste in my mouth that I did not watch the movie until recently, forty years later. *The Babe Ruth Story* was nothing more than another money-making scheme dreamed up by the carpetbaggers who masqueraded as my father's friends. Babe's life story was never given the time and preparation that it deserved because the main concern was to release the movie before he died. And Claire was as much to blame as anyone because *she* approved everything in the film, not my father.

The movie was directed by Roy Del Ruth, but it was Claire who called the shots, so much so that it looked more like *The Claire Ruth Story* than *The Babe Ruth Story*. Claire, played by Claire Trevor in the film, spent most of her time patting herself on the back for successfully molding Babe into a national hero. *She* was the one who told my father that he was telegraphing his curveball by sticking out his tongue. I guess it didn't matter that when Babe was pitching for the Red Sox, he hadn't even met Claire yet. She also "saved the day" by preventing my father, while in a drunken stupor, from visiting a children's hospital dressed as Santa Claus on Christmas Eve. That was a heinous lie. Dad never touched a drop of alcohol before going to a hospital.

Those were only a few of the gross exaggerations. Miraculously, events that in actuality happened years apart in the movie took place on the same day. For example, the day Dad hit his sixtieth home run was the same day he proposed to Claire by sending her the ball with the inscription "Will you marry me?" on it. Dad hit that home run in 1927, two years before he proposed to Claire.

The script was written by Bob Considine, who also worked with my father on his autobiography during most of 1947 and 1948. Even though the book lacked substance due to the fact that Dad was far too preoccupied with his health to concentrate properly, it was still ten times better than the movie. The stilted dialogue, contrived scenes and stereotypical characters made the film more laughable than watchable. Had I not been so close to the subject matter, I'm sure I would have been laughing along with the other people who were watching with me. Some of the more preposterous scenes included Babe ordering a glass of milk in a bar, Babe curing a crippled boy just by waving at him, and Babe carrying on a conversation with Miller Huggins fifteen minutes after the manager had passed away.

Of all the problems with the script, and believe me, there were more than I wish to recount, the worst was the casting of William Bendix as Babe Ruth. Bendix had been a batboy for the Yankees in the 1920s and had met Dad on several occasions. He had great hopes that the role would revitalize his stagnant career. It didn't. Bendix looked more like a caveman, hunched over and swinging a war club. He was right-handed, so it was quite a chore to teach him to hit and swing left-handed, like my father, in such a short period of time. Picture a novice like Bendix trying to emulate the most famous swing in the history of baseball!

Physically, Bendix didn't fare much better. Babe was broad-shouldered and barrel-chested, with spindly legs and a booming voice that filled a room before he himself had actually arrived. Bendix, on the other hand, was short, stubby and whiny. They darkened his hair and fiddled with seventy-five different noses in an attempt to assist the characterization, but it was futile. What bothered me most was that Bendix portrayed Dad as an ignorant wimp.

By his own admission, it was not a film for which Bendix wished to be remembered. "Worst picture I ever made," he lamented. "It could have been great, I think. But it didn't work out that way. I remember going to the previews in Los Angeles. In the early part of the picture, when I'm discovered in the orphanage, the scene is full of sixteen- and seventeen-year-old kids. Do I have a kid playing me? No. I have to do it with makeup. And I'm thirty-eight years old at the time. The audience laughed. I would have laughed, too, but I felt too bad."

Without anything good to say about the picture, my only recommendation is that they retitle it "Ruth-less."

The last two weeks of my father's life were anything but uneventful. While the doctors fought to keep him alive, bizarre events were taking place behind his back. One day I was informed by Babe's doctor that Claire was planning to move him to Mount Sinai Hospital; some doctor had promised that he would add ten years to Babe's life if given the chance. I thought that sounded preposterous, so I asked

Dr. Hayes Martin, my father's attending physician, to show me his X-rays. There was nothing left inside his body. He had half a lung, one kidney and a badly damaged liver.

I asked Dr. Martin, "Can that other doctor possibly replace my father's organs?"

Dr. Martin replied, "Absolutely not!"

When I heard that I was furious. I tracked down Claire immediately and said, "If you try and move his body, I'll have you not only arrested but committed, and I'll have the hospital behind me." Claire simply stared at me in disbelief and didn't say a word.

During my father's stay in the hospital, the *daily* bill came to approximately $900; that included the room, tests, nurses, medications, doctors, everything. I know this will sound strange, but because Babe was "spending"—or "wasting," as Claire saw it—this amount every day, Claire felt that she should be spending the same amount, whether she needed to or not—after all, she had to "live," too.

On top of that, Claire refused to allow Babe's sister, Mamie, a few private moments with her dying brother. After a heated argument in the apartment, I told Claire to "stay put," because I was taking Mamie to see Babe no matter what my stepmother said. When we arrived at the hospital, my father's private nurse was on the phone with Claire; she was telling him to keep us out of the hospital. Thankfully, the nurse did not take Claire seriously and laughed and waved us through. Babe was genuinely pleased to see Mamie, even though her visit lasted an hour, far too long to be good for his health.

On August 11 a bulletin was issued that placed Babe on the critical list. The nation collectively held its breath as updated reports were given on his condition twice a day. The switchboard at the hospital was busy day and night as cards, letters and telegrams poured in by the thousands. A group of little boys collected a cigarbox full of pennies and sent them up to him. Babe was so touched by the outpouring of affection that he insisted on signing as many cards as possible, even though he hardly had any strength left. "We've got to answer everything that comes in," he said. He took a great deal of pride in his autograph and never permitted a plate to be made of it for the purpose of mass production. All autographs from my father were the real thing.

One day when I walked in, a tall, attractive red-head approached me and said, "You must be Dorothy."

I answered, "Yes. Should I know you?"

She replied firmly, "I'm Loretta, your father's girlfriend."

I was astonished, to say the least. Incredibly, I was even more shocked by her next statement: "I certainly hope Babe remembered me in his will. After all, I've given him ten years of my life." I was to find out later that Loretta and Babe had kept close company since 1938. My father has always been accused of being a notorious womanizer. In the position he was in, women were literally throwing themselves at him all the time, but all my father ever wanted was a mate who could share his victories and console him in his defeats. Obviously, Loretta fit the bill. She was his constant companion and catered to his every need—she even went hunting, fishing, boating and golfing with him. I'm glad that at last he was able to find some pleasant female companionship. Lord knows, he deserved it.

In a final outrageous act, my father's will was changed very close to the time of his death, once again because of his so-called friends, who took advantage of his condition. At his death, Julia and I received $5,000 each, while the majority of my father's inheritance went to Claire, most notably his insurance policy. To this day I believe that there was no way my father was of sound mind when he signed that document. I contemplated having the will contested at the time but decided against it when I realized that doing so would only make Babe look bad. I didn't want to see his name in the headlines that way.

It seems that there were a few surprises in store for Claire. Poor Loretta was not one of the lucky beneficiaries and was prepared to make some noise. She threatened to go to the press with details of her and Babe's love affair; her price for silence was $25,000. She had hit Claire where it hurt most: in the pocketbook.

I kept my daily vigil in the nurses' room down the hall. Every day I walked across the street to the church and lit a candle, hoping that the following day he would be gone. I just couldn't stand to see him suffer anymore. After five days on the critical list, he miraculously recovered long enough to receive a few visitors. He got out of bed and walked around for about twenty minutes, even though he wasn't much more than a skeleton. After he went to the bathroom, he was so weak that I had to help lift him back into his bed. He probably weighed less than I did, and I was only about ninety pounds. He told me he didn't want to see Claire under any circumstances.

We talked for a while about how he was feeling, and I asked him once again if he was truly my father. I still had a lot of doubt because the one time he ever admitted it to me was during such a violent argument that he might have just wanted to pacify me. Claire continued to tell reporters that I was adopted, and I had been through so much in my life that I wasn't sure of anything anymore. I needed to be convinced. Babe nodded, and my doubts were once again put aside.

Later that day someone approached me with a photographer. "Can we get a picture of you, Claire and Julia on the front steps of the hospital?" he asked casually. I adamantly refused, telling him to go to hell. Claire and Julia persuaded Mamie to be in the picture.

The following day, August 16, 1948, hospital bulletins once again were given every two hours as my father's condition became progressively worse. At 6:30 P.M. Dr. Martin announced that Babe was "sinking rapidly."

I was in the nurses' room, looking down at the street, when a terrific chill ran through my body. God had finally answered my prayers. At long last he could rest in peace. To avoid the media crunch, I left the hospital through a rarely used side door.

More than a hundred children who were gathered outside the hospital, collecting money for flowers, turned and sadly walked away when they heard the news.

I took the loss of my father very hard, as did the entire nation. My grief was shared by the American people, because in many ways Babe belonged to the public. Many people did not want to believe he had actually died; it was as if they had lost someone in their own family.

President Harry S. Truman was one of the first to offer his condolences. "A whole generation of boys, now grown to manhood, will mourn the passing of the homerun king of the baseball world," he said.

Former President Hoover said, "A small boy once approached me in Los Angeles and asked for my autograph. I gave it to him, but he announced, 'Would you mind giving me three?' I asked him why. 'Because it takes two of yours to trade for one of Babe Ruth's,' the lad said."

The following day, the brothers at St. Mary's Industrial School broke the news to fifty youngsters at morning Mass. Brother Albert, who began his teaching career in 1910, told the boys what Babe had said to him the day he left St. Mary's in 1911 to embark upon a professional baseball career. "We're all in life to do good," my father had said. "And I hope that when I die I will have lived so I can help the boys of America lead cleaner and straighter lives." Most of the boys at St. Mary's had never met Babe or seen him play, but his legacy touched them all and gave them hope for the future.

Babe was originally to be waked at the Universal Funeral Chapel on 52nd Street and Lexington Avenue, but those plans were changed when it became obvious that thousands of mourners would have to be turned away. The funeral director recommended that his body be transferred to a larger place. He suggested Yankee Stadium, and nearly everyone agreed.

Before they took his body to Yankee Stadium I fixed his hair to hide the bandages from the autopsy. I ordered a dozen long-stemmed red roses to be placed on the casket, with the inscription, "All my love to Pop, Dotty." At Yankee Stadium I called to make arrangements to see my father, only to be rudely told by a friend of Claire's that if I wanted to see him I would have to stand in line with the rest of the people.

It still upsets me to think about it. There are still times when I wish there was some way to get even. But then, I've always believed what goes around, comes around. Oh, if I had it to do over again.

In two days, more than 100,000 people passed by his body as it lay in state in the rotunda at Yankee Stadium. The lines stretched completely around the block and lasted until midnight, but anyone who waited was not disappointed because the guards were told to keep the gates open all night if necessary.

One of the first to pay his respects was Peter Sheehy, equipment man with the Yankees and a good friend of Babe's for twenty years. "He was a great guy," Sheehy recalled. "In those pennant-winning days—1926, 1927 and 1928—the groundskeepers and equipment men were not cut in on the World Series money like they are today.

"The Babe, who always used to call me 'kid,' went around with his hat and made all the players get it up for me. He handed me a hundred dollars. I was just a kid and that was big dough."

It's hard to imagine any scene duplicating the one that took place in "The House That Ruth Built." My father's popularity was universal and was reflected in the myriad faces passing his bier: little boys in dirty uniforms, businessmen, secretaries, politicians, teammates, parents carrying infants, people who had seen him play every game with the Yankees, and others who hadn't seen any.

On Thursday, August 19, in a ceremony that was opened to the public, Francis Cardinal Spellman celebrated my father's funeral Mass in St. Patrick's Cathedral. Outside the church, a tremendous crowd estimated at more than 75,000 stood silently in the rain on Fifth Avenue. The only time it stopped raining was when the casket was exposed to the elements: from the funeral parlor to the hearse, and finally from the hearse to the gravesite.

As the procession began, office workers jammed the windows, some making the sign of the cross, and all traffic and construction stopped. You could hear a pin drop in Manhattan. I'll never forget looking out the window of the car and seeing a blind man with his dog. When the hearse went by, the dog went down on his front feet, crouching down with his head bowed between his front legs, as if he somehow knew.

The procession seemed like it would never end. People lined the streets for the thirty-mile trek up Fifth Avenue, through Westchester Hills, all the way to Gate of Heaven Cemetery in Valhalla, New York. My father had not wanted to be buried in the ground in Valhalla; he had requested an above-ground vault in Ferncliff, a cemetery in New York where Claire's mother and brother had been laid to rest. But even his last wishes weren't respected. Once again, his "good friends" had the final say, convincing Claire that Gate of Heaven was the right choice. Every time I think of this, my blood boils.

Even though it has been forty years since my father's death, hardly a day goes by when Babe's name isn't mentioned by one writer or another. And the last time one of my daughters went to visit his tombstone and drop off flowers, the caretaker told her that Babe Ruth's plot is still the one most often visited.

15

The Missing Link

During the 1930s I rarely saw Juanita and Charlie Ellias. They had moved to Jackson Heights, in Queens, about ten miles from Manhattan, and the distance kept them from coming by the apartment as frequently. My father always kept in close contact with Juanita, however, and often visited her on his way to St. Albans to play golf, which he did just about every weekend. Except for taking Babe to the airport in 1946 for his good-will tourist trip to Mexico, Juanita and I went our own ways, until Babe's death in 1948 reunited us. Tragedy has a way of doing that. Juanita and Charlie's presence at that difficult time was very comforting to me, and we subsequently renewed our old ties.

In 1963 life for both of our families changed dramatically. One day, before leaving on a vacation for Florida with Juanita, Charlie pulled me aside and said, "If anything happens to me, please take care of Jenny," his nickname for Juanita. The uncharacteristic remark sent chills down my spine. I wasn't sure how to react, but I tried to reassure him that everything would be fine.

As Charlie was hugging me goodbye, I glanced over at my twenty-year-old daughter, Ellen, who seemed visibly shaken. There was no way she could have overheard what Charlie had said to me, yet somehow she had sensed something.

That was the last time we ever saw Charlie. A week later, a call came in on Ellen's unlisted phone that Charlie had suffered a fatal heart attack while in Florida.

Juanita was completely overcome with grief when she returned from Florida. She had depended so heavily on Charlie for so many years that now she was incapable of managing her own affairs. She had never learned how to write a check or pay a bill, and Charlie had picked out her entire wardrobe because she was colorblind with reds and pinks. But Charlie was more than just her eyes; he was everything to Juanita, and I don't think she ever completely recovered from his death.

Juanita was now faced with the terrifying prospect of living alone in a seventeen-room house on Long Island. She was seventy years old and suffered from dizzy spells; in fact, she had almost fractured her skull during one of them, when she had fallen and hit her head on a radiator. Clearly, she needed someone's help. In 1964 my daughter Genevieve volunteered to take care of her. Juanita quickly became so dependent on Gene, the family's nickname for her, that she did not want to let her come home even for a visit. She was afraid that if Gene left, she might not return.

The following year, Dominick and I decided that the best solution would be for Juanita to move to Connecticut and live with us. It sounded simple, but Juanita could be very stubborn and insisted on having things her way. Instead of her moving to Connecticut, why not have everyone move in with her?

It was one of the most difficult decisions I ever had to make in my life. The sacrifice would be tremendous, but Juanita needed me, and I would just have to make the best of a logistical nightmare: selling our house, adjusting to a new neighborhood, finding new schools for the children—

even separating from my husband. Dominick ran his own automotive parts business in Connecticut, so he remained behind with Richard, living in a trailer, while I took Linda, Gene and Donna and went to Long Island. Ellen and Dan were already on their own.

I was willing to put what I hoped would be a temporary strain on my family for two reasons. First, I had promised Charlie that I would care for Juanita if anything ever happened to him, and I would not go back on my word. And second, Juanita was like a mother to me; she could never do enough for me over the years, and I knew in my heart that it would be wrong to turn my back on her when she needed me most. I doubt that many women would have done what I did, and if I had it to do over again, I probably would have insisted from the start that Juanita move to Connecticut.

The separation from Dominick lasted seven years, from 1965 to 1971. Although Gene and Donna had no problems adjusting to the change, Linda, who was ten years old at the time, had difficulty making new friends and suffered from nightmares for two years. I don't think that she ever felt at home. In 1971 Dominick suffered a heart attack, and we strongly believed that the stress of his driving back and forth to visit every weekend was a contributing factor. Soon after, I informed Juanita, "I'm leaving." This time there was no argument. Juanita put her house up for sale and moved to Connecticut. My conscience was clear.

How can I begin to describe Juanita Jennings Ellias? Eccentric, exotic, elegant, extravagant, fiesty—no list of adjectives can accurately capture her personality. After living with her for seven years, I began to understand the unique characteristics which made her so special, and why she left an indelible impression on all of those who met her.

Every time she came out of her room, it was if she expected to hear someone yell, "Lights! Camera! Action!" Makeup and wardrobe were essential, and careful attention was paid to every detail. From head to toe, she was the epitome of sartorial splendor. She wore lipstick every day of her life, never had a hair out of place, and went to the hairdresser and manicurist once a week. She believed in looking as young as possible and routinely spent two hours a day getting made up. She had cabinets full of perfumes, closets full of clothes, drawers full of pocketbooks and gloves, dozens of pairs of shoes, furs of the most expensive variety. The walls of her bedroom were decorated with pictures of Amazon women, and her wallpaper depicted black panthers and tigers attacking elephants.

She wore hot pants until her mid-seventies and never stopped flirting until the day she died. Her negligees matched her satin sheets, and to watch her go to sleep was the experience of a lifetime: she would fold her arms across her chest and remain that way until morning. If you placed a lily on her lap, she would have looked as though she were being laid to rest. One of her last requests, which we naturally followed, was to have her coffin sprayed with the scent of Chanel No. 5.

In 1978 she had a stroke and was forced to use a walker and wear orthopedic shoes. One day, with her doctor standing outside her room, she entered the hallway without her walker and wearing a pair of slippers. Shocked, the doctor asked, "I thought I told you not to walk around without your shoes!" Juanita snapped back, "I'm not wearing those gunboats, and I'm not coming out of my room again." With that, she turned around and slammed the door.

She would only use her walker when someone was watching; as soon as she was out of sight, she would pick it up and walk without it. We could always hear her scurrying around, but it did little good to reprimand her, since she was going to do things her own way, no matter what anybody said.

I cared for Juanita for fifteen years, from 1965 to 1980, and during that time we had a very special relationship. We were all aware that Juanita had known my father as far back as 1920, and we loved to hear her tell stories of the old days. Naturally, we were very curious to know if she knew who my real mother was. "Your mother was a powerful and influential, well-respected lady who lived in New York," Juanita would say, "and she always loved you. Don't let anyone tell you otherwise." That was the extent of her answer, and despite our prodding and persistence, we were unable to get any further information for many years.

Gradually, she began to drop hints, like pointing out, with a sheepish grin, "Dorothy, we have the same build." And that was it. When she said things like that, I would look at my daughter Linda and say, "Boy, she really is feeling like part of the family!" My children, my husband and I all have brown eyes, the same color as Babe's, except Linda, who has green eyes, the same color as Juanita's. As Linda grew older, she would ask, "How can I have Juanita's eyes when she isn't even related?" I had no explanation for her, figuring that it was just a coincidence.

Then, in 1980, Juanita made a profound statement which changed my life. I was in Cleveland at the time, caring for my husband, who had just undergone bypass surgery. My daughters, Linda and Ellen, along with a nurse, were looking after Juanita in our Connecticut home. Without warning one day, Juanita became hysterical, crying and yelling incoherently. When my daughters finally succeeded in calming her down, Ellen asked why she was so upset. "There is something I have to tell your mother," Juanita said. Ellen waited patiently as Juanita struggled to find the words. Juanita knew the truth was going to hurt. "I am Dorothy's mother!" Juanita whispered.

Ellen and Linda were shocked and assumed that she must be delirious; after all, she was eighty-six years old and very ill. But they soon realized she wasn't. Juanita's actions and speech were deliberate, and her memory was sharp— she was all too coherent and believable. Juanita told them she was afraid that she would die without telling me the truth, and because of that I would hate her forever.

When my daughters told me this bizarre information, I couldn't believe it. I felt betrayed and confronted Juanita immediately. I had cared for this woman for fifteen years, as if she were "my own mother," and had given her everything she needed. Meanwhile, she knew that I was constantly curious about my heritage because I often mentioned it— it had sort of become a family mystery. For so long I had wondered who my real mother was, yet she kept everything a secret. But the bottom line was, at last I had found out the truth.

As we talked, the pieces of the puzzle began to fall into place. Juanita never had had any children of her own, but she did have stretch marks. Her den was filled with 108 pictures of my father, and she often cried whenever she saw them. Also, she always was protective of me and usually took my side during an argument. To top it off, in all the years of our relationship, I had never known Juanita to be a fabricator.

Juanita was extremely weak at the time, but I asked her why she had kept this a secret all this time. She told me that she had wanted to tell me the truth many times, but my father had made her swear never to utter a word. She also explained, "I was afraid that the special relationship we've shared would be lost and that you'd reject me." I appreciated her honesty, but I still longed to know the answers to a thousand questions which had haunted me for years. *Nearly fifty years* was a long time to wait for the truth.

After she finished her story, she felt herself rid of a terrible burden. In less than two weeks, Juanita Jennings, at the age of eighty-six, died of a peritoneal ulcer, commonly known as a "worry ulcer."

Due to the complexity of the story, the cover-ups, lack of documented proof, and the passage of time, I couldn't have possibly expected every question of mine to be answered. With that in mind, what follows is a reconstruction of Juanita's story.

In the summer of 1920, my father was in California for an exhibition tour; while there he had an affair with Juanita. After their brief romance, he left, telling her to give him a call if she was ever in New York.

After a few months, Juanita did give my father a call, but it wasn't from New York. She was calling from California to tell him that she was pregnant with his child. My father assured her that he would take care of everything if she would have the baby in New York. Although she was scared, Juanita felt safe around Babe, so she agreed.

Juanita's parents were outraged at first but relented under one condition: She would have to be accompanied by a chaperone on her journey. The chaperone kept tabs on her as far as New Mexico, but there Juanita evaded him.

Even though my father was married to Helen at the time, he was nevertheless anxious to marry Juanita as soon as she arrived in New York. Juanita refused; "he was too much of a womanizer," and their similarly impulsive, dynamic personalities could not possibly contribute to a happy marriage.

When it came time to have the baby, my father covered all the financial bases: hospital, nurses, furnished apartment, servants and a full-time nanny, Fanny Bailey.

Juanita did not remember the name of the hospital in New York but did recall that she could see water from her window. There was no legitimate birth certificate, because she had the baby under an assumed name. Many reporters tried, but no one was able to trace my birth because of how successfully my father covered his tracks.

After three days, Babe returned to the hospital and somehow managed to leave with both Juanita and me, without any publicity. He was not only married but also in the midst of one of the most phenomenal seasons in the history of baseball, and well aware of what a scandal of this nature could do to his blossoming career. Juanita was single, and women just did not have children out of wedlock. With my father the toast of New York City and undoubtedly one of the most recognizable faces anywhere, it seems incredible that no one was able to find out what was going on. Dad believed that "money talks"; in this case, money probably kept people from talking.

After a year or so of visiting Juanita and me on the other side of town, in the apartment he had designated as our home, Babe decided that he wanted to raise me himself. He figured that he could kill two birds with one stone: Helen would get the baby that she had wanted for so long, and he would be able to see me everyday, without being inconvenienced. Babe told Juanita that he would continue to pay for her apartment on the condition that she give up the baby. He stressed the fact that, since she had no money and was single, there was no possible way for her to raise the baby herself. "I have money and power and I can do whatever I want," he reminded her.

My father made Juanita swear on her life and mine that she would never tell the truth. He also said that if she tried to fight him, she would never be able to see me again. Juanita told me she never forgave him for what he did. "He was a bastard" were her exact words.

Juanita kept her promise and never said a word, but she did devise an ingenious scheme to keep a close eye on me— she became best friends with Claire. Talk about making sacrifices! "That was the only way I could keep the pipeline open between us," she told me. Claire died in 1976 without ever learning the truth.

Juanita told me that a letter was supposed to be read after my father's death that would explain everything. The letter never appeared, so I only have Juanita's word.

In recent years there has been one additional piece of evidence that I believe corroborates Juanita's story. In 1923 a famous photograph was taken of my father sitting on a hospital bed and holding hands with Helen. Helen is wearing an exquisite, three-diamond ring on her left hand, which is unmistakably the same ring I now have in my possession—a ring given to me by Juanita Ellias.

She told me that Babe had sent her the ring on one of the stems of a dozen long-stem roses. According to Juanita, he could be very romantic when he wanted to be.

16

Number Three Was One of a Kind

People have constantly referred to my father as "one of a kind." Another favorite phrase is "There'll never be another Babe Ruth." And quite possibly the most common description of all has been "They threw away the mold when they made Babe Ruth."

Those familiar quotes were probably meant more figuratively than literally—but maybe not. In 1921 Johansen and Holmes of Columbia University performed an extensive laboratory study on the psychological behavior of my father; Professor B. Pitkin of Columbia in 1930 interpreted the results as part of his book, *The Psychology of Achievement.* Professor Pitkin's exhaustive analysis of data gives new credibility to some of baseball's oldest and most overused cliches concerning my father.

"Consider the rarity of Babe Ruth," wrote Professor Pitkin. "Not even the most enthusiastic fan has ever appreciated that this home run genius is, in the strictest statistical sense, far rarer than one man in a million . . . . Most of the tests were of the ordinary sort, designed to measure his quickness of motor responses by way of eye and ear, his strength, his nervous stability, his attention span, and his general coordination in manipulating objects.

"Babe Ruth scores 90-percent efficient in his general co-ordination, as against the 60-percent score which most men score in the same tests. His eyes function 12-percent faster than normal; and in his nervous stability, he is so superior that he surpasses 499 out of every 500 persons.

"Babe Ruth's eyes are the best of five pairs. His ears are the best of five pairs. So his combination of eyes and ears is the best out of 25 men. His general attention is the best out of 100 men. So, the combination is the best out of 2,500 citizens. His nervous stability is the best out of 500 men. So the combination of this with the preceding sets of traits makes him the best out of 2,500 x 500, or 1,250,000 people. And we still have to reckon with his amazing muscular strength.

"Underneath all of this we find, as the solid foundation of his physical genius, an amazing basic metabolism. Had we the figures on all these characteristics, we should find that Babe Ruth, far from being 'a man in a million,' is at least one man in 50 or 60 million. Were men paid according to the scarcity of rivals who can do their work equally well, Babe Ruth should be receiving at least 10 million dollars a year."

I can just picture my father walking into Jacob Ruppert's office with Pitkin's findings and demanding to renegotiate his contract. The year this study was completed, Dad was in the first year of a two-year contract at $80,000 per year. With or without scientific data, I think it's safe to say that Babe Ruth was one of a kind, and that encompasses a lot more than hitting the long ball.

The popularity of home runs and the frequency with which Babe hit them overshadowed his versatility as a complete ballplayer. He was not a one-dimensional player, and he often won games without the aid of his bat. Besides his remarkable success as a pitcher for the Boston Red Sox, he also had good range as an outfielder, an accurate throwing arm, and better-than-average speed on the basepaths.

His eyes were so keen that he could read the license numbers on an automobile when it was so far away that others could not even make out the colors of the plate. In his first four years with the Yankees, he stole fifty bases, and ten of those were steals of home.

In talking to many of his old teammates and friends, I notice that fielding is the one facet of his game that they most frequently talk about. Joe Sewell played third base for the Yankees from 1931 to 1933 and was on the receiving end of many of my father's throws from right field. "If there was a base hit to right field, with a man on first base, all I had to do was put my glove between my feet and the ball would take one bounce and land right in the middle of it," remarked Sewell with a smile. "He was the greatest throwing outfielder I ever played with, and I played with Speaker. Others may have had a strong arm, but Babe's was more accurate. You can have a strong arm, but if you're not accurate with it, you might as well throw it straight up in the air."

"I never saw him make a mental error," recalled Ben Chapman, left fielder for the Yankees from 1930 to 1934. His old friend Johnny Vander Meer said, "He was never given credit for his fantastic baseball instincts. He never threw to the wrong base or missed a cutoff. He had that God-given baseball instinct to do the right thing. There've been a few others, but he was probably the master of them all."

No player ever captured the imagination of fans the way my father did. Not to take anything away from the great New York Yankee teams, but the fans came to see Dad, and they would not leave until he took his turn at bat in the ninth. People would often say, "Hey, Mike! Going to see the Babe play today?" It wasn't, "Are you going to see the Yankees?" or the Red Sox or any other team. "When the Babe came to town, there were 50,000-plus fans; when he left, there were 4,000," remembered Hall of Fame umpire Jocko Conlon. "He really packed them in," said Mark Koenig, a shortstop and teammate of Babe's. "He really *made* baseball."

My father did more than just change the strategy of the game with the advent of the home run; he also changed the conservative mentality of the game. Baseball had been staid; tipped hats, blown kisses and animated encores were not part of the game until he came along. Babe Ruth was Mr. Baseball, and he wore the title as a king wears a crown. He owned the crowd and used its energy to raise his performance an extra notch. The fans inspired him. The louder they applauded, the higher he lifted his hat. He lived his life under a microscope, and with Babe's bulk, it was almost impossible to go anywhere without being mobbed. Hall of Fame catcher Bill Dickey, a teammate of Dad's for many years, remembered the wonderful effect he had on people. "We were riding through my home town in Arkansas on a train," recalled Dickey, "when all of a sudden the train comes to a halt. Do you know, the people in town found out Babe was on that train and had it flagged down?"

"He could always wave the right way or say the right things," said Johnny Vander Meer.

"He used to drive around in this sixteen-cylinder Cadillac that had to be close to thirty feet long," laughed Lefty Gomez, holding up one hand and pointing all the way across the room with the other. "One day, Babe and I were racing through the Catskills. There happened to be a policeman parked on the side of the road who recognized Babe and yelled, 'Hi ya, Babe!'

"Well, I'm right behind him, and as soon as the cop sees me, he flags me down for speeding. Babe saw what happened, whipped his car around and came to my rescue. 'It's okay, officer,' he said confidently. 'He's with me.'"

Dad believed baseball was the fans' game, and if home runs were what they wanted, he would do his best not to disappoint them. In one game against Cleveland, he got five hits in five times at bat but was booed loudly for not hitting a home run. Fortunately, for the most part he was able to hit home runs as if it were the most natural thing in the world to do, so the fans usually got their money's worth and then some.

He loved nothing more than putting on a good show, but at the same time he was a careful student of the game. My father may have appeared undisciplined and lackadaisical in his approach to baseball, but, knowing him, that was probably part of his act. "Don't let the stories about the Babe fool you for a minute," exclaimed Vander Meer, chuckling. "He knew what arm you threw with. He knew everything about you."

Dad was a fierce competitor. When he stepped into that batter's box, nothing was going to break his concentration. "When he put on that uniform, he was going to beat somebody," Sewell told me emphatically. "He was a winner, and if you weren't in high gear all the time, you were in trouble."

Babe was proud of his accomplishments but not overly concerned with them. He owned the spotlight but did not treat the players he overshadowed as inferiors. In fact, Dad's most cherished award was the one he received from the *New York Evening Graphic* for clean sportsmanship. Joe Sewell remembered one particular game at Yankee Stadium: "I got five hits in five times at bat against Lefty Grove, and I was a left-handed hitter. My fifth hit that day was a home run into the right-field stands.

"Up until this point, Babe had failed to hit a home run. I'll never forget Babe waiting for me at home plate. He shook my hand and said, 'Well kid, they all came out to see me hit a home run today, and you picked me up.' He was a tremendous team player who thought a lot of his fellow man."

An important aspect of my father's life which sometimes gets overlooked was that he was even more of a team player *after* he left the ballfield. There was much more to life than hitting home runs and winning pennants, he felt, and he could make a difference in the overall lives of people, many of whom society had ignored or treated as outcasts. He would go to Atlantic City to visit injured war veterans and spend days walking around, talking to the paraplegics. These trips upset him a great deal, and when he came home he would always say, "They'll never get a chance to see me if I don't see them."

Another story that received no publicity was his tour of a leper colony on the Hawaiian island of Molokai. Friends tried to convince him that the trip would be dangerous, and that he would be at great risk, but he ignored their warnings and ended up spending most of the day talking, playing ball and eating lunch with the island's inhabitants. Some of the lepers did not speak English, but language barriers were no match for the Babe's big smile, open arms and colorful personality. I remember asking him when he returned if he had been afraid, and he answered simply, "If God wants me to catch leprosy, then so be it." My father was more than a great man, he was a great humanitarian.

Mamie Ruth told me that she always remembered him "smiling, laughing, and full of the devil." Ben Chapman said, "He didn't take himself too seriously. He was always fooling around in the clubhouse. One time he actually locked Jimmy Reese in a locker."

"Babe loved to have fun," his old pal Lefty Gomez fondly agreed. "He had a heck of a sense of humor and was probably one of the game's greatest pranksters. One day he cut the toes out of Tony Lazzeri's socks. Tony got even by cutting one of the legs off Babe's uniform. Luckily Babe had another uniform in the car, but he had to walk through the crowd with one pant leg missing.

"One of his favorite tricks was to put a worm in the finger of your glove and wait for your reaction. Other times he'd crack an egg and put it into your shoe. He thought that was the funniest thing in the world. But of all his pranks, his classic one was with tobacco. His aim was uncanny. He'd be sitting four or five guys away from you on the bench and still be able to arch a mouthful of tobacco right smack on your shoe. He perfected it, like a basketball hook shot."

My father always lived life as if the next moment might be his last. He loved life and respected death, but neither was meant to be taken seriously. For example, Mamie remembered the first time Babe brought me to see her. He was standing on her front steps, holding a laundry basket containing a neatly wrapped infant! "This is my new baby, Dorothy," he exclaimed.

Dad found living on the edge exciting, and often amusing. One day he was sitting in the clubhouse at St. Alban's golf course, taking practice with his .22-caliber rifle; he and a friend were shooting at the doorknob for a dollar a shot. Without warning, a man opened the door, and Dad missed hitting him by six inches. The near victim was scared half to death, while Dad remained totally unfazed. His tongue-in-cheek reaction: "He should've knocked."

Not everyone was amused with his antics, particularly the Yankee triumvirate of general manager Edward Barrow, manager Miller Huggins and owner Jacob Ruppert. Dad knew how to have a good time and scoffed at those who tried to stand in his way. The Yankee management tried to place restrictions on Babe's lifestyle, which resulted in some of baseball's classic confrontations. There were fights, fines, suspensions and holdouts. Babe didn't believe anyone had a right to tell him how to conduct his life when it came to baseball. Ben Chapman once said, "I've heard people say the Yankees had one set of rules for Ruth and another set for everyone else. That's not true. There were no rules for Ruth."

Whatever rules existed, Babe did his best to break them. He would do things without thinking about who might be offended or what the consequences might be. After the damage was done, he would hang his head and plead for forgiveness, usually from one of his chief adversaries. And despite all the grief he caused Barrow, Huggins and Ruppert, he still remained in their good graces, somehow managing to redeem himself to each one of them in his own inimitable way. Miller Huggins once said, "He's given me more headaches than the rest of the team combined, but next to Lou Gehrig I like Babe better than any player I've ever known."

When Ed Barrow retired in the mid-1940s, he said, "What I'll miss most about baseball is the big fellow. He caused me more trouble than any three people I've ever known or come in contact with, but he's still number one in my affection."

And when Colonel Ruppert was on his deathbed at the age of seventy-one, he requested to see Babe. My father went to the hospital and tried to lift Ruppert's weakened spirits. "You're gonna snap out of this," he whispered, leaning over the bed, "and you and I are going to see the opening game of the season." The colonel could only smile faintly and squeeze my father's hand before passing away.

Upon hearing the news that my father had passed away, Barrow said, "One of the saddest things in life is to outlive one of your children. The Babe was one of my children, you know, baseballically speaking."

My father once had a rather unique experience with Colonel L'Hommedieu Tillinghast Huston, Ruppert's partner with the Yankees. Babe convinced Colonel Huston in 1922 that the fairest way to determine his salary for the next three years was to flip a coin. Huston flipped the coin and lost, and Dad's salary, which had been $30,000 the year before, jumped to $52,000 for each of the next three years.

Although Babe's salary was eventually to reach $80,000, his disposition was not altered by the almighty dollar. As Mamie pointed out: "Money all too often goes to people's heads, but I don't think that was ever the case with George. He was just as nice to a poor person as he was to his rich friends. He never forgot anybody who needed help."

Babe had a very cavalier attitude towards money, especially when it wasn't his own. For example, he had a number of funny financial exchanges with Lefty Gomez, who was a rookie in 1930. "He'd tell me how much money to sign for and when to sign the contract. The funny thing was," said Gomez, finding it hard to believe even fifty-seven years later, "that right after I finished signing my name, Babe would start laughing and say, 'Gomez, you dope! Why didn't you hold out a little longer? You could've gotten more money!'"

Another time, Gomez got his contract in the mail, and Dad ripped it up without even looking at it. "You're not signing that," he said.

Lefty nervously responded, "But Babe, I'll lose my job."

"No problem," Dad laughed. "I'll take care of it."

Babe's supreme confidence was not limited to salary negotiations. Lefty told me that whenever he was pitching, Babe would stop by the mound on his way out to the field and say, "Just keep 'em under five runs. I'll take care of the rest."

Back in 1914, when my father was a rookie with the Boston Red Sox, he began to throw his weight around. A rookie was the low man on the totem pole and had to earn the right to take extra batting practice, but Babe was oblivious to this unwritten rule and took as many swings as he wanted; as a result, he challenged three of Boston's veteran stars: Tris Speaker, Duffy Lewis and Harry Hooper. They did not find his cockiness amusing and proceeded to teach him a lesson by sawing all of his bats in half.

Not all of the anecdotes about my father are quite so humorous, but I really feel the problem has been that too much literary license has been taken with the truth, making it difficult to separate fact from fiction. It's a shame that some writers have felt compelled to tarnish his image with gross distortions of reality, such as eating an eighteen-egg omelet for breakfast and twenty-four hot dogs in one sitting, or going to bed with an entire whorehouse in one night. "It really hurts me to read some of the stuff that has been written about Babe since his death," said Lefty Gomez. "I guess when you're in the public eye, there are people who will try and dig up dirt about you."

I don't think it has as much to do with being in the public eye as it does with being a legend who was larger than life and whose actions often defied logical or reasonable explanation. Let's face it, exaggerated stories about Babe's life have been constant grist for the rumor mill. Sensationalism sells. Babe Ruth eating eight hot dogs is no big deal, but twenty-four—now there's a story! I don't mean to be overly critical; for the most part, the writers have been more than fair and genuinely dedicated to keeping my father's memory alive. I do hope that in the future less is made of his locker-room-style behavior and more is made of his on-the-field accomplishments.

One of these accomplishments, Babe's "called" home run in the 1932 World Series, remains one of baseball's most cherished stories. More than a half century later no one is really certain whether or not he pointed his bat toward the center-field bleachers in Wrigley Field. Dad relished that home run above all others because of the bad blood that existed between himself and many of the Chicago Cub players throughout the World Series.

The feud had started before a pitch was even thrown. Just before the Series began in New York, the Yankees learned that the Cubs had voted to give shortstop Mark Koenig only a half share of their World Series proceeds. Koenig had been a productive player for six seasons with New York, and although he had been traded to the Cubs earlier in the year, he was still friendly with many of his old teammates, including my father. It was true that he hadn't played a full season with the Cubs, but he did hit .353 in 33 games and was their regular shortstop when they won the pennant. Dad felt that the Cubs were treating his friend pettily and had no intention of letting them off lightly. He delighted in calling the Chicago team "cheapskates," "pennypinchers" and some unprintable expletives.

The bench jockeying in New York, where the Yankees won the first two games, was mild compared to the unmerciful verbal assaults before Game 3 in Chicago. Being the most outspoken Yankee, he practically waged a personal war against them. Dad could trade insults and obscenities with the best of them, but when a group of fans spit on Claire as they walked arm-in-arm into their hotel in Chicago—that was going too far.

Babe quieted the jeers in the first inning when he stroked a three-run shot into the right-field stands. The Cubs bench howled derisively as he crossed home plate. The Yankees led 3-0. Ruth 1, Cubs 0.

In the fifth inning, with the score tied at 4-4, Dad stepped into the batter's box amidst a chorus of boos, hisses and catcalls. A couple of lemons were even hurled in his direction. After working the count to two balls and two strikes,

Dad challenged over 50,000 screaming fans, an incensed, half-hoarse Cubs bench, and a fuming Charlie Root, who was waiting impatiently on the mound, to lay the next pitch over the plate.

Whether Dad pointed toward center field with his bat, raised a finger on his right hand and waved it at Root, or simply said to catcher Gabby Hartnett, "It only takes one to hit," the result was one of the deepest home runs in the history of Wrigley Field and one of the most stunned crowds in World Series history.

With the passage of time, it no longer matters much what really happened that day; what matters is that people are still talking about it. Stories like these are the reason why the legend of Babe Ruth will stand the test of time.

To analyze my father is a complex task. Much of what has been written about him would lead one to believe that he was a simple man. He wasn't. The public Babe Ruth was the antithesis of the private Babe Ruth. He had two completely different personalities. At home he was solemn and would not say much at all. Conversation was limited mostly to arguing over Claire's drinking problem. There was a constant feeling of uneasiness, as if a time bomb were hidden under the bed. An explosion would come; it was just a matter of when.

Yet for some reason he tolerated Claire's every demand. He could be so communicative with total strangers yet so distant from his own family. He didn't have trouble telling Ed Barrow or Miller Huggins what was on his mind, but he did have trouble telling me. The public knew my father as an emotional, uninhibited individual: rejoicing after home runs, arguing with umpires, and weeping openly at the funerals of close friends. Part of the reason he was more open in public, I'm sure, was because he kept his emotions bottled up at home.

Dad did not have close ties with his parents and never had the opportunity to learn what primary relationships were all about. Since he didn't experience a normal childhood, his fear of being close to me, on a one-to-one basis, may have been something he didn't even notice. No doubt he was apprehensive about saying the wrong thing to me, so he dealt with his insecurity by retreating into a shell and not saying anything at all. He wasn't the ideal parent, but even when he tried to be, Claire thwarted his efforts.

When Dad finally left St. Mary's Industrial School for good, people remarked that it was as if a caged animal had been set loose. The same analogy can be applied to the way his disposition changed whenever he left the apartment. He was spontaneous and wanted to sample everything life had to offer. Babe was no saint, but then he never tried to be someone or something that he wasn't.

17

Baseball Remembers the Babe

Jimmy Reese, Babe's room-mate with the Yankees in 1930:
    I went with Babe to visit St. Mary's, and they took us in-to a room with straps lined up against a wall. They said, "These are the straps we used on Babe Ruth."

Ben Chapman, Yankees outfielder, 1930-1934:
    It was always in the paper and I agreed with them: "As Babe goes, so go the Yankees." In other words, he was the bell cow.

Mark Koenig, Yankees shortstop, 1925-1930:
    He had such a beautiful swing, he even looked good strik-ing out.

Lefty Gomez, Yankees pitcher, 1930-1943:
    I think it's safe to say that no one hit home runs the way Babe did. They were something special. They were like homing pigeons. The ball would leave the bat, pause brief-ly, suddenly gain its bearings, then take off for the stands.

Eliot Asinof, author, Eight Men Out:

When I was eight years old, my father would take me to Yankee Stadium. I distinctly remember Babe Ruth hitting home runs early in the game, prompting about half the fans to head for the exits. All they wanted was to see Babe Ruth hit a home run.

Ben Chapman:

I don't think anyone hit 'em as far as Babe did. He was the first one to put a ball into orbit.

Joe Sewell, Yankees third baseman, 1931-1933:

One day we were playing in St. Louis, and Babe hit one across Grand Avenue and on top of a three-story building. I was on first base and I stopped before I got to second to watch it. That was the farthest ball I ever saw him hit. It must have been a half-mile high.

Bill Dickey, Yankees catcher, 1928-1944:

I saw him hit balls so high to the infield that nobody wanted to catch them. The players would fall down and Babe would end up with a triple.

Joe Sewell:

When Babe hit sixty home runs in 1927, no one even pitched to him. I played for the Indians back then, and we threw the ball in the dirt, behind his back, over his head, anywhere but over the plate. If everyone pitched to him, he would've hit 100.

Ben Chapman:

The farthest home run I ever saw him hit was in Birmingham. It went completely out of the stadium and over the railroad tracks. I've never seen anybody hit a ball like that. You couldn't measure most of Babe's, because they went 475 to 500 feet on the average. If he were playing today, he'd hit 90 home runs.

Babe Ruth:

We were playing an exhibition game in Chattanooga, and I hit one ball that landed in a freight car. Later that day someone found the ball about twenty miles from the stadium, in the freight car. Now that's one Mr. Ripley can use in his book anyday.

Mark Koenig, about Babe's third home run in the third game of the 1926 World Series:

The pitcher had Babe struck out, but the umpire ruled the pitcher had "quick-pitched" him or something, so he called it a ball. Wouldn't you know, Babe hit the very next pitch into the right-field stands for his third homer of the game.

Bill Klem, home-plate umpire for the third game of the 1926 World Series:

The three home runs Babe hit in that game were the three farthest balls I ever saw hit.

Ben Chapman:

I remember him hitting that first home run in the 1933 All-Star game, because I replaced him in the outfield that day. He hit that one about nine miles.

Mel Allen, Yankees broadcaster, 1930s-1980s:

The first time I saw Babe Ruth play was in Detroit against the Tigers. I was only a teenager at the time, but I'll never forget that day.

The Yankees were trailing by about five runs when Babe made the final out in the top of the eighth inning. After the Tigers were retired in their half of the eighth, Babe ran in from the outfield and sat on the *Tigers* bench: laughing, knee slapping, and having a good time. You really weren't allowed to sit in the opposing dugout, but the umpires let it go because it was Babe.

Well, in the top of the ninth, the Yankees stage a big rally and bat around. All of a sudden it's Babe's turn to hit again. The bases were loaded when he stepped to the plate and hit the first pitch deep over the center-field fence. The Yankees scored six runs or so in the inning and went on to win the game. I'll never forget how Babe laughed like crazy as he ran around the bases.

Joe Sewell, about Babe's "called shot" in the 1932 World Series off the Cubs' Charlie Root:

I was looking right at it. I had just hit a ball to right center field that Hack Wilson caught. I went back to the bench and sat down next to Sammy Byrd. Babe was up at the plate clowning around. He didn't say a word to Charlie Root, not a word. But he was cussin' at Burleigh Grimes, Bob Smith and Guy Bush on the Cubs' bench.

After he got one strike, Babe held up one finger at Burleigh Grimes. Then he got a second strike, and he held up two fingers. He then got out of the batter's box with the bat in his left hand and pointed with two fingers toward center field. He got back into the batter's box, and on the next pitch—I still have a mental picture of that ball leaving the ballpark. You know how a golf ball takes off? Well, that's exactly how that ball took off.

It went right through a tree in center field that was filled with little boys. Sammy Byrd, who was sitting next to me, said, "Look at all those kids falling out of the tree!" The boys were all going for the ball. As Babe rounded third base, the fans started throwing lemons, cabbages, eggs, oranges and even umbrellas. The game had to be stopped for fifteen minutes to clean the field. Nobody can tell me that Babe didn't point. He did.

Ben Chapman, regarding the same day:

The Babe was at bat, and Charlie Root knocked him down. When Babe got up, he pointed toward the pitcher's mound, in the direction of center field, and then hit the home run. When he came into the dugout, someone asked him if he called his shot. Babe answered, "No, but I called Root everything I could think of."

As far as I'm concerned, that's exactly what happened. When he went into the clubhouse after the game, all the writers asked him if he called his shot. Babe replied, "Well, certainly I called it."

As you know, Babe was quite a showman, and Mr. Baseball, and he wasn't going to miss an opportunity like that.

Babe Ruth—the final word?:

I took two strikes, and after each one I held up my finger and said, "That's one and That's two." Then's when I waved to the fence!

No, I didn't point to any spot, but as long as I called the first two strikes on myself, I hadda go through with it. It was damned foolishness, sure, but I just felt like doing it and I felt pretty sure Root would put one close enough for me to cut at, because I was showin' him up. What the hell, he hadda take a chance as well as I did or walk me!

Gosh, that was a great feeling, gettin' a hold of that ball and I knew it was going someplace. Yessir, you can feel it in your hands when you've laid good wood on one. How that mob howled. Me? I just laughed, laughed to myself going around the bases.

Yeah, it was silly. I was a blankety-blank fool. But I got away with it, and after Gehrig homered behind me, their backs were broken. That was a day to talk about.

Billy Hermann, Cubs second baseman, 1931-1941:

He didn't point, don't kid yourself. If he'd pointed, do you think Root would have thrown him a strike to hit? I'll tell you what he would've done. Remember, he was ahead on the count. Right—you guessed it—Ruth would've been sitting in the dirt, maybe rubbing himself where it hurt.

Gabby Hartnett, Cubs catcher, 1922-1940:

Babe waved his hand toward our bench on the third base side. One finger was up, and he said quietly—and I think only the umpire and I heard him—"It only takes one to hit." Root came in with a fast one, Babe swung, and it landed in the center-field seats. Babe didn't say a word after the home run. If he had pointed out at the bleachers, I'd be the first one to say so.

Bill Dickey:
I know the true story—I was in the on-deck circle with Gehrig at the time—but I'm gonna hold my tongue.

I used to get in arguments with Gabby Hartnett. He'd say, "Ruth did not point." And I'd say, "Oh, yes he did, Gabby. Oh, yes he did." And he'd get so mad at me he couldn't see.

Let's just leave it like that.

Jimmy Reese:
In one game against Cleveland, manager Tris Speaker had Babe walked with the bases loaded, two outs, and his team only leading by two runs. That's how much they thought of Babe.

Hank Greenberg, Tigers first baseman, 1933-1946:
I had the good fortune of playing two years against Babe Ruth. He was in a class by himself. He overshadowed [Jimmy] Foxx, Gehrig and the rest of them. Ruth was the only player I knew that when he came out on the field, everybody stopped. It was like the star came on center stage. When he went to take batting practice, nobody looked at anything but Babe. When you've got that type of magnetism, you know you're the star.

Bill Dickey:
When he'd take batting practice, both the opposing team and his own team would drop everything just to watch him swing. To have that kind of control over your teammates, you know you're something special. No matter how many home runs anyone ever hits, you'll never see another Ruth.

Bob Lemon, Indians pitcher, 1941-1958:
When I was twelve years old, I played hooky from school and rode my bicycle fourteen miles to Long Beach, Califor-

nia, just to get Babe Ruth's autograph. After the exhibition, in which Babe hit about two dozen balls out of the park, he was signing balls in the parking lot. I couldn't believe who was standing next to him waiting for an autograph—my father. I rode like hell to get home before he did.

In later years we used to practice with that ball when Dad wasn't around. He kept looking at it from time to time and wondering why the name on the ball kept fading.

Bill Dickey:
I was scared to death of Ruth and Gehrig. I was trying to hit the ball as far as them, and I could never do that as long as I live. Miller Huggins came up to me and said, "You're trying to hit the ball as far as Ruth and Gehrig, aren't you?" I said, "Yes sir." Huggins then told me to get an Earle Combs model, choke up on the bat, and hit to all fields. It really helped me.

Jimmy Reese, regarding one of the inconveniences of rooming with Babe:
I couldn't sleep because the phone rang all night long—and none of the calls were for me. In the middle of the night, Babe would come strolling in the room and say, "What's goin' on?" I'd respond, "Oh, nothing, except that I have about four hundred phone messages for you."

Pat Olsen, a long-time friend of Babe's:
I remember Babe staying out one night real late, and Huggins promising to slap a heavy fine on him for breaking curfew. Babe somehow evaded Huggins the next day and went four-for-four in the game, prompting Huggins to say, "What the hell are you gonna do with a guy like that?"

Lefty Gomez:
One time we were driving through puddles in St. Petersburg when Babe's car stalled because the wires were soaked. You know who ended up pushing that car to the gas station? Me! Babe sat behind the wheel and laughed, "Faster, Gomez, faster!"

Bill Dickey:

I came into the clubhouse one day and my shoes were nailed to the floor. The only guy there was Tony Lazzeri, and he told me Babe had done it. Back in those days shoes cost sixteen dollars a pair, which was a lot of money. I was a rookie and really didn't know what to do.

The next day I bought myself an egg and put it in one of Babe's shoes. Everyone in the clubhouse knew what I was up to and waited anxiously for Babe to come in. We all watched as Babe got dressed, and, wouldn't you know, the last thing he put on was the shoe with the egg in it. You could see his face clearly, as he looked around in disbelief. He turned the shoe upside down and emptied the egg out onto the floor. He got really mad and turned red. Then he walked to the opposite end of the clubhouse looking for the guilty party.

Well, I called out in this little fine voice, "Babe, I put that egg in your shoe." He turned around real fast and came running right up to me. I thought he was gonna take a swing at me, but all of a sudden he broke out in a big laugh, and all you could hear was laughter throughout the clubhouse.

Jimmy Reese:

We were scuffling in the clubhouse one day before a ball-game when Babe decided to lock me in a locker.

It so happened that he hit a home run that afternoon. He came up to me and said, "Well, you're going in the locker again tomorrow." He did that for three consecutive days, because he hit a home run all three days. It got to the point where I was hoping he wouldn't hit one out of the park, because I was getting tired of being locked in that locker.

Ben Chapman:

I had some disagreements with Babe because he would always make me play the sun field. If it was right field, then I played there. If it were left, then I played there. I really didn't mind as long as I was getting to play every day.

Jimmy Reese:

We were playing pool one night in his apartment, and he owed me twenty dollars. Mrs. Ruth comes in the room and says, "Babe, dinner is ready." Babe said, "I can't go until I get even." After he won the next game, he said, "Okay, now we can eat." He just didn't like to lose.

Another time, he wouldn't let Lou Gehrig go to sleep until he got even in a game of bridge.

Johnny Vander Meer, Reds pitcher, 1937-1949:

He may have had a hang-up on names, but he had a fantastic memory for faces and places. If he went by a road or a town once, he wouldn't need a road map the next time. He had an incredible memory from eyesight.

Jimmy Reese (about Babe's golf game):

He could hit the ball four hundred miles, but he had no control. They said they shouldn't charge him green fees, because he never used the course.

Joe Sewell:

I was in New York the day they retired his uniform. Babe came into the clubhouse with his attendant, and I turned and said to my son, "Go over and get a good look at him, because he's not going to be with us much longer." He died about three months later.

Dr. Bobby Brown, Yankees infielder, 1946-1954, and current president of the American League, about Babe Ruth Day at Yankee Stadium:

His body had been ravaged by cancer, and you could tell that death was imminent, which made that day at Yankee Stadium a sad one. He almost had to speak in a whisper, which made it very difficult for everyone to hear and understand what he was saying. It was a tragic sight, involving someone you always thought was indestructible.

Happy Chandler, Commissioner of Baseball, 1945-1951:

After the 1947 meeting of the owners at the Waldorf Astoria in New York, they told me Babe was in Lenox Hospital, very ill. None of the other baseball people went to see him. They had neglected him and refused to give him a job. They knew he was dying, but it was of no concern to them.

Babe was lying in bed as I walked into the room. As soon as he recognized me, he held up his left arm. It was so sad to see him that way. His arm was so brittle and shriveled up. He turned his head into the pillow and cried like a baby. I stayed with him for about fifteen minutes. Later that year I got him a job with the Ford Motor Company.

Lefty Gomez, regarding Babe's final days in the hospital:
When Babe was dying of cancer, I remember total strangers stopping in front of the hospital to say a prayer for him.

Mel Allen:
Many people have told me that the reason they brought their infants to see Babe, as he lay in state in the rotunda of Yankee Stadium, was because one day they wanted to tell them they saw the great Babe Ruth.

Jocko Conlon, Hall of Fame umpire:
He did more for baseball than any man in the twentieth century.

Babe Ruth:
Baseball is the only truly American game, and every American boy should play it.

In 1986 Yankee pitcher Joe Niekro was fined ten dollars by a team kangaroo court for endangering a historical treasure. Niekro had thrown the pitch that Kirby Puckett hit off the Babe Ruth Monument at Yankee Stadium.

18

The Babe Ruth Scrapbook

The Babe Ruth Scrapbook was conceived in 1976, shortly after the death of Claire Ruth. I was busy cleaning out Claire's apartment when, quite accidentally, I discovered stacks upon stacks of old, discolored newspapers piled up to the ceiling in a closet. I stopped in my tracks, sat down on the floor and started flipping through the brittle pages. My eyes lit up as though I had just opened a treasure chest—it was the find of a lifetime.

One of the first headlines I turned to was from the *Daily Mirror*: "Babe Ruth Is Dead." I remembered seeing that headline almost thirty years before, but to see it again, under those circumstances, sent chills down my spine. As I anxiously turned the pages, Dad's entire career flashed before me: "Ruth Hits 60th Home Run," "Did Ruth Call His Shot?" "Ruth and Gehrig Lead Yankees," "Babe Calls It Quits." I wished I could have continued reading them all day but the landlord had told me that everything had to be cleared out of the apartment that afternoon. I didn't have a huge car, but I made the most of my trunk space; I have to assume that whatever I left behind was thrown down the incinerator. I felt as if I had just robbed a bank and made a clean getaway.

When I got home, my daughter Linda and I started the tedious job of going through all the newspapers to compile the articles for a scrapbook. Finding a scrapbook large enough to accommodate our needs was almost as difficult as the task itself. After scouring through art-supply stores for weeks, we finally found what we were looking for: an enormous black beauty, about two feet long by three feet wide and weighing in, unfilled, at about thirty-five pounds.

The herculean chore of meticulously cutting and pasting each article into the scrapbook took us three straight days, from ten o'clock in the morning to twelve o'clock at night. Dominick and my son-in-law, Andy, provided moral support, offered "helpful" hints like "Don't forget to dot the 'i's' and cross the 't's'," and told us when a clipping was crooked. At the end of each night, we looked as if we had gone swimming in an inkwell or worked in a coal mine. Our hands were black from the newsprint, our hair was white from the ink we used on the black scrapbook pages, and our faces were covered in paste.

By the third day, the living room was in complete disarray, with scraps of newspapers covering almost every piece of furniture. On top of that, we were both delirious. I'm surprised one of us didn't cut off a finger and paste it in the scrapbook! When the book was finally finished, we knew how the Egyptians felt after they had built a pyramid.

The Babe Ruth Scrapbook is one of our family's prized possessions; its value could not possibly be calculated in dollars and cents. The personal contents, such as fan letters, canceled checks, financial statements, income tax stubs, and original newspaper clippings from as far back as 1919, make this family heirloom irreplaceable.

The following pages are some of my favorite excerpts from this scrapbook.

Babe Ruth
at age 3 yrs.

The famous
favorite Raccoon
Coat

My Dad, the Babe   221

Bambino Does His Farming in the Winter Time

Here you see the world's greatest slugger in uniform and as he looks upon his farm in the winter season. At top, in the center, Ruth with Mrs Ruth and their daughter, Dorothy, on his farm at Sudbury, 20 miles outside of Boston. Below, Babe as a teamster hauling logs on the farm.

owd Predicted for Ruth Games This

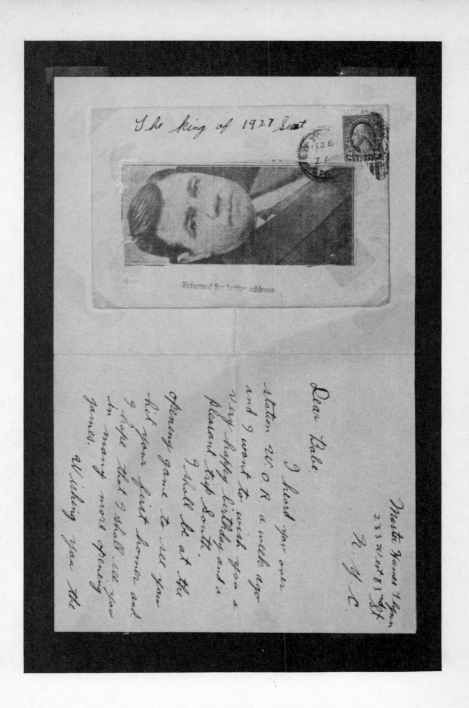

The king of 1927 Swat

Returned to better address

Martin Manon & Gym
233 West 83 St
N. Y. C.

Dear Babe

I heard you were
sicker W. O. R. a week ago
and I want to wish you a
very happy birthday and a
pleasant trip South.

I shall be at the
opening game to see you
hit your first homer and
I hope that I shall see you
in many more gerning
games.

Wishing you the

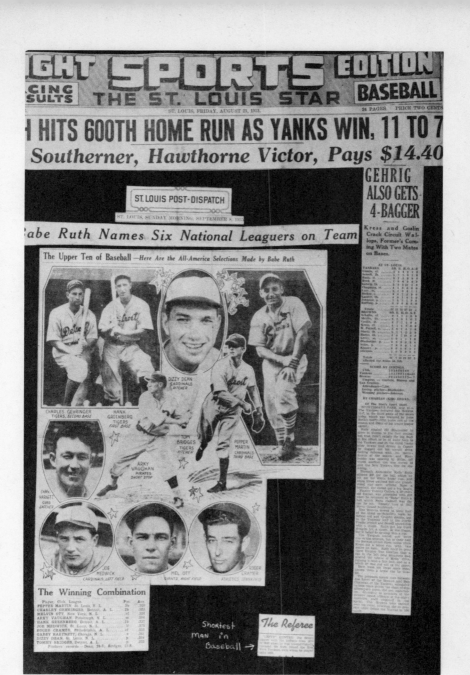

RACING RESULTS

NIGHT SPORTS EDITION
THE ST. LOUIS STAR
BASEBALL

ST. LOUIS, FRIDAY, AUGUST 21, 1931.   24 PAGES   PRICE TWO CENTS

RUTH HITS 600TH HOME RUN AS YANKS WIN, 11 TO 7
Southerner, Hawthorne Victor, Pays $14.40

ST. LOUIS POST-DISPATCH
ST. LOUIS SUNDAY MORNING, SEPTEMBER 8, 1935

Babe Ruth Names Six National Leaguers on Team

GEHRIG ALSO GETS 4-BAGGER
Kress and Goslin Crack Circuit Wallops, Former's Coming With Two Mates on Bases.

The Upper Ten of Baseball —Here Are the All-America Selections Made by Babe Ruth

CHARLES GEHRINGER — TIGERS, *Second Base*

HANK GREENBERG — TIGERS, *First Base*

DIZZY DEAN — CARDINALS, *Pitcher*

TOM BRIDGES — TIGERS, *Pitcher*

PEPPER MARTIN — CARDINALS, *Third Base*

ARKY VAUGHAN — PIRATES, *Short Stop*

GABBY HARTNETT — CUBS, *Catcher*

JOE MEDWICK — CARDINALS, *Left Field*

MEL OTT — GIANTS, *Right Field*

ROGER CRAMER — ATHLETICS, *Center Field*

The Winning Combination

Player, Club, League	Pos.	Avg.
PEPPER MARTIN, St. Louis, N. L.	3b	.320
CHARLEY GEHRINGER, Detroit, A. L.	2b	.383
MELVIN OTT, New York, N. L.	rf	.328
ARKY VAUGHAN, Pittsburgh, N. L.	ss	.394
HANK GREENBERG, Detroit, A. L.	1b	.332
JOE MEDWICK, St. Louis, N. L.	lf	.378
ROGER CRAMER, Philadelphia, A. L.	cf	.328
GABBY HARTNETT, Chicago, N. L.	c	.341
DIZZY DEAN, St. Louis, N. L.	p	.304
TOMMY BRIDGES, Detroit, A. L.	p	.222

Shortest man in Baseball →

The Referee

Needlepoint
Silk Tapestr
Presented by
Japanese peo
1934
(Hand sewn)

Nakanishi E.W.C. Laboratory
Fukuoka Japan

228 **My Dad, the Babe**

Babe Ruth died of cancer at 8:01 last night at Memorial Hospital
Two Full Pages of Pictorial Biography on Center Fold.

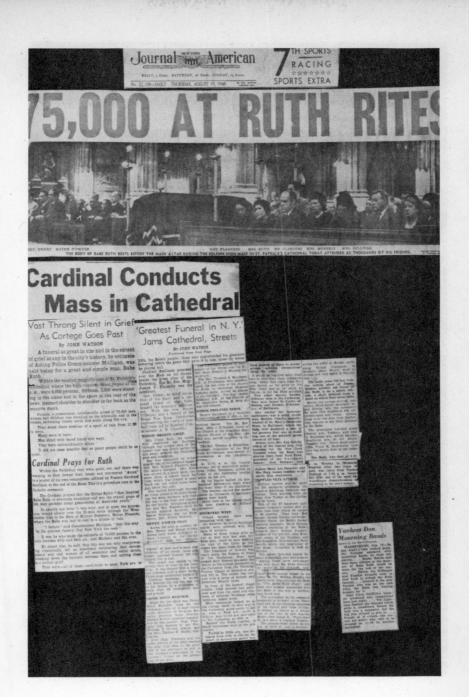

CITY EDITION DAILY NEWS 3¢

Copr. 1948 by News Syndicate Co. Inc. NEW YORK'S PICTURE NEWSPAPER Trade Mark Reg. U. S. Pat. Off.

Vol. 30. No. 48   New York 17, Friday, August 20, 1948*   60 Main + 4 Manhattan Pages   3 Cents IN CITY | 4 CENTS | 5 CENTS

RUTH'S LAST GATE
HIS GREATEST

Story on Page 3

Harry Escobar, 3, in mourning for the Babe, looks on solemnly as Mr. Baseball is carried from Lexington Ave. chapel.

Bell Tolls for Ruth
In Cathedral Mass

By Arthur Mulligan and Harry Schlegel.

Ave. and 53d St. Hurrying pedestrians paused to bare their heads as the funeral party rolled north through Manhattan and into the Bronx.

Pass East of Stadium.

At 161st St. and Grand Concourse the hearse paused only a few blocks east of Yankee Stadium, the steel and concrete pile fashioned by the Babe's slugging bat, where more than 100,000 filed by his bier Tuesday and Wednesday.

All along the route to the cemetery in Hawthorne little knots o...

DAILY NEWS 3¢

New York 17, Wednesday, August 18, 1948

50,000 PASS RUTH'S BIER

The House that Ruth Built opens its doors to the Babe for his last visit.

Thousands Bid Babe Good-by at Stadium

By William Martha and Henry Lee

In The House That Ruth Built with the mighty bat, in the great arena which he triumphantly christened with a home run on opening day, the kids,

Fans jam sidewalk action from Universal Funeral Parlor, 52d St. and Lexington Ave., to watch the casket of Babe Ruth start on its journey to the Stadium.

the fans and the great public filed sadly past the Babe's thinned form last night.

Youngsters stride stonily past Babe's bier after long wait in line to pay respects to man whom they came to idolize although they'd never seen him in action. Estimated 6,000 persons per hour passed bier.

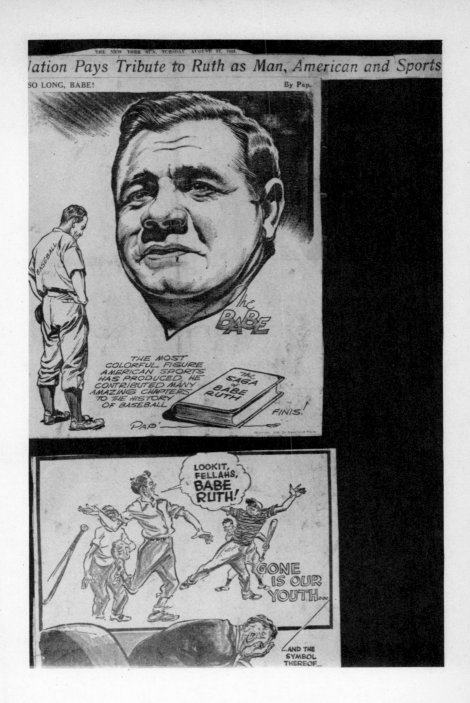

HIS LAST HOME RUN. By Rube Goldberg

238   My Dad, the Babe

Dan Parker

Rookie Scribe of 1925 Recalls 1st Trip with Babe

ST. PETERSBURG, Fla., March 5.—

IT'S 32 YEARS since the Yanks opened their training camp in this special place in the sun and the same length of time since this peregrinating paragrapher made his first Spring training trip. Many things have happened in the intervening period—half the average life span—but nothing can erase the memory of that first pilgrimage with the Yankee club of Babe Ruth's boisterous heyday.

I hit the jackpot right off the bat by being assigned to accompany Babe Ruth to Hot Springs, Ark., for several weeks before proceeding with him to St. Petersburg. The trip was to end suddenly for Babe in the railroad station at Ashville, N.C., on the journey northward in an incident that made headlines across the nation, had America worried about its prodigal son for weeks and probably cost the Yankees the 1925 pennant.

Babe, who had just celebrated his 30th birthday as he left for the Arkansas Spa to boil out, was in his roistering prime as Col. Ruppert's beloved problem child. Accompanying me on the trip to Hot Springs was Marshall Hunt, the veteran writer, of the Daily News, now editing a newspaper in the Northwest. Everett Scott, the original Yankee Iron Man, who was getting along in years, was also sent down to boil the stiffness out of his creaking bones before tackling his last season as the Yanks' shortstop.

I HAD BROUGHT ALONG a newspaper camera to get some pictures of the Babe and, the morning after our arrival, timidly asked him if he'd be so kind as to jog up a steep country road leading to the hills.

"Sure," said Babe. "Let's go," and off we went, Babe setting a good pace and your correspondent, lugging a heavy Graflex, trying to keep up with him. Halfway up the mountain road, there was a souvenir photo shop with rearin' broncos, deader than Mr. Kelsey's great grandfather but stuffed in the most "rarin' to go" poses imaginable. Babe mounted one of the critters, donned a cowboy's hat and chaps, grabbed a rope and gave with some blood curdling yipee-eye-ohs while the neophyte cameraman blundered through a series of double exposures, slide-covered shots and other such crimes against Daguerre, Eastman and the rest.

Resuming his road work after this pause, Babe was nearing the top of the hill when he suddenly keeled over. As I tried frantically to get the camera in focus and ready for a shot, Babe turned around, as he lay on the ground panting, with a "When are you going to take it?" expression that stampeded me into tripping the lever before pulling out the slide. Then Babe arose and brushed himself off. The incident left me wondering whether Ruth was the most cooperating subject on earth or had really suffered a weak spell and dropped from exhaustion. I asked Marshall Hunt about it and, as an expert on Babe through several years of following the Yanks around the American League. He took the cynical view that the Yanks' star hitter was thinking of Ed Barrow, general manager of the club and the only man in baseball whom he feared.

"He wants to show Cousin Ed he's training hard down here instead of carousing," said Marshall. On the homeward trip some weeks later I was to do a double-take on Babe's flat Springs swoon and do some wondering. In later years, after getting to know the Babe better, I probably came up with the real answer. Ruth was the kindest hearted guy in the world to anyone who was breaking in and I swear now he toppled over on the Hot Springs hillside that February morning in 1925 just to provide a rookie baseball writer with a good picture and something to write about.

IF THE TRUTH must be told, Babe didn't fake his training too seriously at Hot Springs, where a good time was to be had by all, but he did dunk himself daily in the hot mineral baths at one of the old hotels on the main stem where it started to go uphill. The hotel was full of fighters and their managers—Jock Malone, the St. Paul middleweight, and Leo P. Flynn, of New York, among others. Tris Speaker had his Cleveland Indians batterymen in town for a bit of early training that year and they worked out in a ramshackle old ball park. Beautiful spring weather prevailed until the last day of our stay in Hot Springs. Then a howling blizzard swooped down from the North and there was over a foot of snow as we pulled out for St. Petersburg that evening.

St. Pete was a village of about 15,000 permanent residents in 1925 but a land boom was in progress that saw building lots, covered with palmetto and infested with rattlesnakes, changing hands four or five times daily, at fantastic advances in price, with some of the fleeting owners never even laying eyes on their property. Walter Hagen was the pro at a suburban development called Pasadena which had a fine golf course. The Yanks stayed at the Princess Martha Hotel, then the best in town. The Ku Klux Klan paraded now and then along the main stem to keep the carpet-baggers in line. Casey Stengel, in his last season as a major league player, was with the Boston Braves in St. Pete that

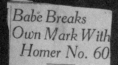

Babe Breaks Own Mark With Homer No. 60

Circuit Hit Wins Yanks' Game As Fans Fight For Ball

YANKEE STADIUM, New York, Sept. 30.—Babe Ruth, king of home runs, put another star in his crown this afternoon.

With a mighty clout, he drove out his sixtieth circuit hit of the season in the eighth inning of the Yankees' game with the Senators. When he finished trotting around the bases he had broken his own record, established in 1921, of 59 homers.

Besides his own run, Ruth drove in Mark Koenig, breaking a 2 to 2 tie and enabling the Yankees to win, 4 to 2.

Tom Zachary of the Senators is the pitcher whose name will be remembered in connection with the Bambino's 60th home run of 1927. The Babe had been up three times before, walking once, while the crowd howled its disapproval. Twice he caught hold of good pitches, but only singles resulted.

His Big Chance

Then, in the eighth, with the score 2 to 2, Ruth's big chance came. Combs, first up for the Yanks, was tossed out by Bluege. Mark Koenig rattled a triple off the left field stands.

The crowd sensed the approaching drama as the Babe stalked up to the plate, seriously tapping his cleats.

THE POWERHOUSE
By Jimmy Powers

All too soon all of us who ever saw Babe Ruth play baseball will die and then, one by one, the little screens of memory will fade. One could compare the human mind to a newsreel with the innermost vault of the brain imprisoning childhood reels, color pictures of adolescent scenes, and highlights of maturity complete with recordings of familiar voices. Performances are run at will. There is no admission fee. It is all so much better, and certainly more soul-satisfying than the flat, ghostly, one-dimensional commercial celluloid. Yes, assuredly there will come a day when no one alive will remember Babe Ruth. Then it is only a question of the accumulated dust of centuries until he is forgotten entirely and for all time.

It is a sobering and humbling thought and it explains perhaps some of the pathetic and well-intentioned suggestions that reached our sports desk the past 24 hours via telegram, special messenger and telephone. Some fans wanted the old Bambino deposited under the green sod of right field. Others urged fantastic monuments, charity drives, or a rash of new

R VLSUS VUVL

ed from page 1)
)-year-old slugger hit the
Nixon phoned his con-
n was in left field when
rough but talked to the
innings.

for the record many
ble was surrounded by
hich Baseball Commis-
in had intervened twice.
ed Atlanta to play Aaron
e opening road games at
— after the slugger had

tied the record Thursday with No. 714 — ordered the Braves to play Aaron in the final
road game Sunday.

✈ The legendary Ruth played for 22 seasons,
got into 2,503 games and had 8,399 at-bats in
hitting 714 home runs. The softspoken Aaron
is in his 21st season, and the record-breaker
came on his 11,295th at-bat in his 2,967th
game. ✈

The home run also brought Aaron across
the plate for the 2,064th time in his career, a
National League record

include a 120-piece marching band f
previously performed at the Super Bow
national anthem and present the colors.

The mammoth Babe Ruth League p
program, will fly over Yankee Stadium
dent Case and Mrs. Babe Ruth will p
George Steinbrenner with a handsome lif
Bambino in appreciation for their genero
program over a period of years. The pa
artist Pete Boruta — widely acclaimed f
and portraits of many government offici

The painting has been previewed for th
of the National State Bank on West State
were distributed to all of their branches.
vice president of the bank and Command

he MORNING RECORD
APRIL 9, 1974

Q. *A man of gross appetites, Babe Ruth was never
involved in a bedroom scandal. How come? Was he
sterile?—Dan Nevitsky, Chicago.*
A. Babe Ruth was lucky. In his early days he was involved in a couple of paternity suits, but nothing
came of them. The circumstances concerning Dorothy, daughter of his first wife, Helen, have never
been completely revealed. She referred to Dorothy
as adopted, but others believe she was issue of Helen
and Babe Ruth. One of the best biographies of Ruth
is *Babe* by Robert W. Creamer (Simon and Schuster).

*Parade
Magazi
(Sunday Su
1978*

**BABE RUTH AND DAUGHTER DOROTHY
AT THE 1928 WORLD SERIES**

eeted
Today

ed him money. Ruth
ore than he was, and
nt outranked him.

ling the Big Man's
Fuchs to Ruth and
Ruth to McKechnie
from McKechnie to
s—all sounding as
een written by Fuchs
vo will go great to-
mil." the president
er, whose dour face

ew his players would
sence, no matter how
e been. They did,
clared, "He made all
American League, so
ay there?"

gel, Brooklyn's man-
"I just hope he don't
ague calling his shots
nst the Cubs in the

Vithout Dane

m

SPORTS

Co

By MILTON
ATLANTA (U
ron expected t
controversy, and
There is alread
The luster is s
new home run r
isn't preventing
from continuou
that Hank Aaro
2,900 more offici
than Babe Ruth
That number w
minish and so
ment that Aaro
compare with R
home run hitter
knows he'll kee
more and more
the years, and
fact of life
Likewise, he's
heard the last ye

Many papers are philosophizing because Babe
Ruth refused to accept a salary of $75,000 a year.
"What are we coming to," they wish to know, "when
a mere ball player scorns the salary we pay our
President?" The answer is that we pay our cooks
and don't pay our wives. Those who can hope for no
reward except money must be paid in money, but
there are services for which money can't pay. Imag-

240   My Dad, the Babe

19

Life After Babe

As I sit here writing this, it's hard to believe that forty years have passed since my father's death, and over that time the name Ruth has remained in the headlines. Newspaper polls and write-in contests such as "Baseball's Classic Moments," "The Greatest Athlete of the 20th Century," "The Greatest Baseball Player of All Time" and others have helped keep his memory alive. For me it's like he never left. Sometimes I think that at any moment he will come driving down the street or walking in the door.

Shortly after his death, I had a difficult time. Almost daily I was reminded of Babe. My health began to fail, and I was completely exhausted. According to my doctor, the excessive weight loss which I was experiencing was due to severe stress. He suggested that Dominick and I go on a vacation.

In most cases families try to forget about the death of a loved one, put it behind them, and go on with their lives: giving clothing to charities, placing pictures in boxes, selling sentimental items, or even locking a room. Anything to make the transition easier. However, coping with the death of someone as celebrated as my father required a totally different approach. Think of what it would be like to receive phone calls and mail every week for forty years concerning the death of a member of your family. It was a difficult adjustment for me, but rather than try to suppress his memory, I have always embraced it.

From 1948 until the mid-1970s, I remained out of the public eye, living a quiet, suburban life, mostly in Connecticut, raising a family and breeding horses on a farm that I named after my father's, "Home Plate Farm." During that time, Claire did a creditable job of steadfastly carrying on my father's tireless interest in baseball by traveling around the country promoting Babe Ruth Baseball, the largest competitive baseball program for players between the ages of six and eighteen currently operating throughout the United States and Canada. The organization had been established in 1952 by Marius Bonacci.

In 1976 Claire Ruth died of cancer at the age of seventy-six. Her death, in her Manhattan apartment on Riverside Drive, was a painful one; she was heard screaming for a preacher in her last moments. Because I had not seen her for quite some time, I was unaware of her condition. The week that she died, I had tried to get in touch with her. The first time I called, Julia told me Claire was shopping. The second time, she was supposedly in the bathroom. And the third time I called, Julia informed me that Claire was sleeping. I finally realized that I was getting the runaround, so I stopped calling. Two days later, Julia called to tell me that Claire had died. I hadn't even known she was sick.

After Claire's death, I accepted the responsibility of carrying on the time-honored tradition of Babe Ruth Baseball. I became its spokesperson, and one of my first responsibilities was to give a speech in front of a large audience. I was petrified. I had never spoken into a microphone, and the thought of it caused my knees to knock.

I will never forget that first speech, if I can call it that. When I started "talking," nothing came out—I mean, not a *word*. People were looking around, wondering if something was wrong with the microphone, but I only wish the problem had been that simple. Mercifully, the audience was very patient, enabling me to eventually relax. After I regained my composure, I was able to utter a few syllables, so the evening wasn't a total embarrassment.

I have also spent the last ten years trying to uphold the family name. This has proven to be no easy task. At times it has been necessary to call sportswriters and broadcasters to complain about things they have said or written. I don't enjoy admonishing or reprimanding other adults, but if they insist on fabricating stories, then they leave me no alternative.

In recent years my itinerary has been hectic but rewarding. My father had so many plans for working with youth, but because of his illness he never had a chance to see his dreams reach fruition. Dad laid the foundation; now it's up to people like me to build the house. I'm very proud of Babe Ruth Baseball and all those connected with it. The four divisions total 23,000 teams, 433,000 participants, and over a million volunteers who manage, coach, take tickets and run the concession stands. It simply amazes me to see how much the organization has grown, and how many children are involved. Every so often one of the boys makes it to the major leagues. At last count, 233 graduates are now in the big leagues, including some of the game's brightest stars: Don Mattingly, George Brett and Dale Murphy, to name a few. Now that's what I call progress! Babe Ruth Baseball continues today as a living memory of and tribute to my father.

At the 1978 Babe Ruth World Series in Newark, Ohio, I was escorted by Babe Ruth World Series President Richard Case, his last act as president before turning over the reins to Ron Tellefsen. I have attended other tournaments in Babe Ruth Baseball's home state of New Jersey, as well as Rhode Island, Maryland, Connecticut, and Jamestown, New York. And each year I attend the opening of the league in Wallingford, Connecticut.

No matter where I have visited, the people have always gone out of their way to make my stay a pleasant one. The hospitality shown to me has really been moving. On one occasion, in Jamestown, I rode in a parade down Main Street in my father's 1922 Pierce Arrow. I'll never forget all of the reporters asking, "What was it like to ride in that car in 1922?" What could I tell them? I was only an infant at the time.

When I travel around the Babe Ruth Baseball circuit, my duties are usually limited to throwing out the first ball, giving speeches, doing interviews or signing autographs. I sign as many autographs as I possibly can, but I don't have anywhere near my father's endurance. Following in his footsteps, I also try to visit orphanages and children's hospitals, no matter how sad the setting. I now understand how much those visits used to upset Babe; I've been reduced to tears on several occasions myself.

Undoubtedly, being the daughter of Babe Ruth has opened many doors for me and given me the opportunity to meet many fascinating people. In 1981 I was invited to the National Portrait Gallery in Washington, D.C., at the request of Nancy Reagan, for the opening of "Champions of American Sport." I met President Ronald Reagan after he gave a speech, honoring the one hundred champions who were chosen. Many of sport's greatest stars were on hand: Oscar Robertson, Willie Mays, Jack Kramer, Gordie Howe and Bill Russell, to name a few. Besides myself, there were also descendants of Jesse Owens, Jackie Robinson, Duke Kahanamoku, Hawaii's most proclaimed surfer, and others. Over the years I've even had the pleasure of meeting relatives of Confucius, Geronimo, Abraham Lincoln, Rocky Marciano and Admiral Perry!

One of the most exciting events each year for me is Old Timers Day at Yankee Stadium. My father's name is still pure magic. When I'm introduced I always get goose pimples. The rafters shake, and the deafening applause sometimes lasts for three or four minutes. I almost feel as if the ground is ready to open up. Old Timers Day never gets old for me.

My other annual pilgrimage is to the Baseball Hall of Fame in Cooperstown, New York, for the induction ceremonies every summer. Since 1962 I've only missed one year; it's important to me to show people that I still care. I have made my children promise that when I die, one of them will continue to represent the Ruth family at the event each year.

During Hall of Fame Weekend, Cooperstown is transformed from a sleepy, pastoral town into a vibrant community. Time has a way of standing still for those three or four days. Many of my old friends, such as John Mize, Joe Sewell, Lefty Gomez, Pat Olsen and others, journey from different parts of the country to relive their baseball pasts. In a way the Hall of Fame Weekend is our Fountain of Youth. Sometimes the same old stories get "better" with age; the ball may travel a little bit farther or the pitch a little bit faster, but the stories are just as sweet. Once in a while I'll go to the Hall's Babe Ruth Exhibit and browse along with the baseball aficionados, studying their reactions and eavesdropping on their conversations. Cooperstown gives me that rare opportunity, once a year, to turn back the hands of time.

I've also accepted numerous awards on Babe's behalf, such as the one I received from the Boston Red Sox for Dad being voted their all-time left-handed pitcher. The Red Sox "Dream Team" was selected by the fans and sponsored by the Gillette Razor Corporation.

On July 6, 1983, at the All-Star Game in Chicago, the United States Postal Service issued a twenty-cent stamp in honor of Babe. Fifty years earlier my father had hit the first home run in All-Star competition, at Chicago's Comisky Park.

I was also in Baltimore for the dedication of my father's birthplace as the Babe Ruth Shrine and Museum. And on September 10, 1986, the Canadian Baseball Hall of Fame unveiled a color lithograph depicting Babe's first professional home run, hit in 1914 at Toronto's old Hanlan's Point Stadium. Babe was a pitcher for the Providence Grays when he clouted that home run against the Toronto Maple Leafs of the International League. They only printed 714 lithographs, the same number of home runs Dad hit during his major league career.

Recently I am attempting to see that my father is awarded the Presidential Medal of Freedom, the highest civilian award presented by the U.S. government. The medal is awarded for meritorious contributions to the security or national interest of the United States, efforts towards world peace, or cultural or other significant public or private endeavors. The President bestows the honor at his discretion to either civilians or members of the military, to natives or foreigners. If Babe recieves the award, he would share the honor with football coach Paul W. "Bear" Bryant, baseball great Joe DiMaggio, actor James Cagney, astronaut Neil Armstrong and musician Duke Ellington, just to name a few.

I sincerely believe that my father deserves the award for many reasons. He was a goodwill ambassador to Hawaii before it became a state, as well as to England and Japan. As I have said already, as far as I'm concerned he saved the game of baseball—the national pastime—so that it continues to be enjoyed by millions every year. To this day he has an impact on the youth of America; he is listed in encyclopedias and written up in school textbooks.

Yet being the daughter of Babe Ruth has not only brought awards, bouquets of flowers and standing ovations. There has been a negative side. For many years I was so paranoid that I told my children not to admit to being Babe Ruth's grandchildren, because I feared someone would kidnap them in order to demand exorbitant ransoms. The abduction of the Lindbergh baby was always in the back of my mind, so I proceeded with extra caution. When my daughter Linda grew older, she began to tell her friends that Babe Ruth was her grandfather, but no one believed her until I gave her some autographed pictures of Babe to prove it.

For some strange reason, people are thoroughly convinced that I am a very wealthy woman and call me from time to time, wondering if I could lend them money. It's true that I have lived a comfortable life, but not because of any money inherited from my father. It's been my husband's hard work and dedication to his family that has enabled us to be financially secure.

I also receive strange phone calls from collectors who would like to know if I've grown tired of Dad's memorabilia and would like to sell anything. On the other hand, there have been a few rare instances where people have called and offered me baseball cards and pictures of my father because, as they put it, "Babe Ruth's family should have them." It's certainly refreshing when that happens. And, as funny as it seems, people somehow think that I have unlimited World Series tickets! Just like most fans, I pay for every ticket I receive.

Through the years, various priceless heirlooms of Babe's have vanished, the most upsetting of which was the disappearance of most of his World Series rings. Unfortunately, incidents of that nature have caused me to be much more guarded around strangers. Collectors have obtained numerous items of my father's, courtesy of Claire: uniforms, jewelry, clothing, bats, golf clubs, fishing equipment—you name it. Customarily, family heirlooms are passed down from generation to generation; they should *not* be in the hands of private collectors. Even personal gifts which I bought for my father are in the hands of strangers. I resent this very much! Claire gave away or sold my family heritage. These items may not have meant much to her, but they mean a great deal to me. Babe is *my* father, and my children's grandfather, and now a great-grandfather to my grandchildren.

When the play *The Babe*, starring Max Gale as my father, opened on Broadway a few years ago, I wasn't even aware of it until the last minute; in fact, I found out about it by watching a TV talk show. When I called Max Gale, he told me that the producers of the play had told him that Babe Ruth had no living family members. He was shocked to hear from me and seemed genuinely upset that we hadn't had a chance to meet, because he felt that the character he was portraying was incomplete. He had researched Dad well, mostly from books and old news footage, but was unsure of certain idiosyncrasies, such as Dad's walk, laugh and mannerisms. I believe he felt cheated. I explained that I would have been more than cooperative had I been contacted earlier, and then I presented Mr. Gale with a personally autographed Louisville slugger. To show his appreciation, he used it in the show. He did a wonderful job, so much so that at times I almost forgot that he wasn't really my father.

One of the most aggravating days of my life was April 8, 1974—that's the day Henry Aaron hit an Al Downing fastball over the left-field fence in Atlanta's Fulton County Stadium for his 715th home run. That home run was a bitter pill to swallow, much the same as Roger Maris's 61st home run in 1961. I did not feel that Aaron had broken Dad's career home run record, and I called Phil Pepe of the *New York Daily News* to voice my opinion with the following prepared statement. "I'm not minimizing what Aaron did. He hit more home runs than my father and I admire him for it, but he did not break my father's record, because he played in so many more games." I feel that same way today. Aaron played in 798 more games and batted 3,967 more times! My father hit a home run approximately every nine times at bat. If he batted the same amount as Aaron, he would have hit 1,154.

When Aaron hit that historic home run, my phone never stopped ringing. Reporters were hounding me for my reaction, but for the most part I refused to comment. One reporter was so intrusive that he even went so far as to stick his foot in my front door. Finally I screamed, "Talk to Mrs. Ruth. *She'll* give you a comment!"

For once, Claire and I were in agreement. She wasn't thrilled with baseball's new home run record, but she was less adamant about it than I was. A few weeks later, as a sign of good faith, Claire graciously agreed to meet Mr. Aaron on the field at Atlanta's Fulton County Stadium for a formal presentation of an artist's painting of my dad. Aaron chose to stay in the clubhouse while Claire waited patiently on the field.

Through it all, I've learned to accept the good with the bad. I've tried to be cooperative with the media, answer fan mail, and spend time on the telephone with high school students doing book reports. More importantly, though, I've tried to be a good mother and wife. My family is extremely important to me, and I insist on having all my children together for the holidays. I've taught my children not to use their tie to Babe Ruth as a crutch to gain special favors—I never wanted them to think that they were any different than anyone else.

My father has been and will always be an important part of all of our lives. For my family, there is no escaping his legacy. Almost every room in our home has something that belonged to my father. My prized possession is his grand piano, which cost $3,000 when he purchased it in 1929. I'm also proud of a huge urn and a giant poster which were presented to him when he toured Japan. There's also a wooden plaque, which I love, bordered by sixty baseballs and symbolizing his record-setting home run year of 1927.

Babe's presence can really be felt in the downstairs den, which is decorated much the same as the Babe Ruth Exhibit in the Hall of Fame. I have autographed pictures and baseballs from players ranging from Grover Cleveland Alexander to Honus Wagner. I also have a rare team picture signed by every member of the 1927 Yankees.

When I'm in a nostalgic mood, I walk around and study my father's facial expressions in some of the pictures or just read the inscriptions. There are a couple pictures of the two of us that are of great sentimental value. In one, he's holding a bat in his left hand and has me balanced comfortably on his right shoulder. Some of the photos may be faded, but the memories of the happy times we spent together will always remain sharp and clear in my mind. Had the circumstances been different, maybe we would have been closer. I've often wondered what our relationship would have been like if I were a boy. . . but certain questions were never meant to be answered.

I loved my father very much, but I didn't realize just how much until after he passed away. It's not that I took him for granted; I just misplaced my priorities. I was only twenty-eight years old when he died, and I dare say that I had a lot to learn about life. I thought that I would have a lifetime of second and third chances to try and strengthen the bond between us, but his tragic illness curtailed any long-range plans I may have had.

I am very proud to be Babe Ruth's only child and believe that he would be equally proud of the work I've done in his name. In an eerie sort of way, that work has brought me closer to him in death than I was ever able to get in life. More than ever, I love my dad, the Babe.

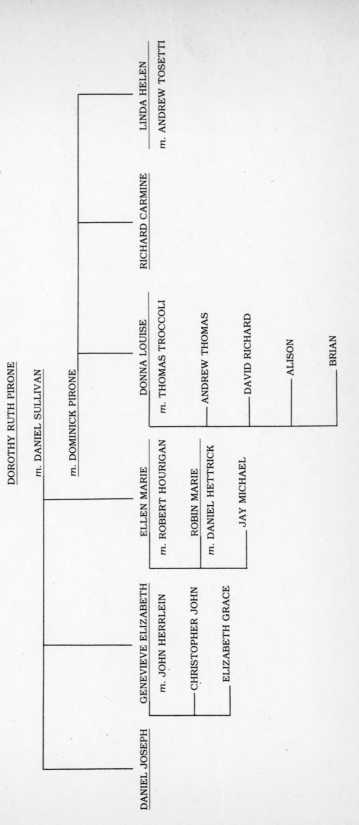